All the New

New

IRA

Roth • Traditional
Educational

How to cash in
on the new
tax law changes

Steve Merritt, MBA

First Edition

Halyard Press, Inc.
Melbourne, Florida

© 1998 by Steve Merritt

Published by:
Halyard Press, Inc.
P.O. Box 410308
Melbourne, FL 32941-0308
407-634-5022; Fax: (407) 636-5370

Printed in the United States of America

Publisher's Cataloging-in-Publication
(Provided by Quality Books, Inc.)

Merritt, Steve.
    All about the new IRA : how to cash in on the new tax law changes / by Steve Merritt. --1st ed.
    p. cm.
    Includes index.
    ISBN 1-887063-07-2

    1. Individual retirement accounts--Popular works.
I. Title.

HG1660.U5I72 1998   332.024'01
                      QBI98-456

Dedication

To my loving wife, Sandy, who supported me through count-
less hours of research and analysis as this book was prepared.
It is truly a blessing to find one person who is a partner, best
friend, wonderful mother and loving wife.

Table of Contents

Note to the Reader   **9**

1. The New IRA Will Put a Smile on your Face   **11**
How Many Kinds of IRA's are There Anyway?

2. All About the Traditional IRA   **15**
Tax-Deductible IRA vs. Non-Deductible IRA • Examples of Contribution
Eligibility • How to Get Money Into Your IRA • How to Keep Track of
Taxes • Conduit IRA • IRA Distributions • Distributions Before Age 59 1/2
• Distributions Between Age 59 1/2 and 70 1/2 • Distributions at Age 70 1/2
and Older • Penalties for Excessive Withdrawals • Rollovers and Transfers •
Estate Planning • Investments Allowed in an IRA • How to Start an IRA •
How Many IRA's Can You Have?

3. All About the Roth IRA   **43**
How the Plan Works • Basic Features • Are You Eligible? • Examples of
Eligibility • Distributions • Rollovers • Converting an IRA to a Roth IRA •
Estate Planning • Tax Corrections Bill • Do State Taxes Apply? • How to
Start a Roth IRA • Investment Opportunities • Roth vs. Non-Deductible
IRA • Roth vs. Taxable, Non-IRA Investment • Roth vs. Deductible IRA •
Benefits of Roth IRA • Investments that Work Well In a Roth IRA

4. The Educational IRA   **69**
Basic Features • Trust Agreement • Are You Eligible? • Distributions •
Rollovers • Things to Consider • Investment Tips • How to Start an Educa-
tional IRA • Strategies and Implementation

5. Create an IRA Strategy that Works   **85**
401(k) vs. the IRA • Strategy is Important • Non-Deductible IRA Has Lost
Its Appeal • Tax Brackets • How Will You Use Your IRA Funds? • How
Far Are You From Retirement: • After-Tax Cash Flow • Other Tax-
Deferred Investments • Real-Life Ways to Use an IRA • Convert or Not to
Convert • Borrowing from Retirement Vehicles

6. What You Need to Know About Investing   **109**
Minimize Investment Cost • Seek Investments that Fit Your Risk and
Return Profile • Implement Your Investment Selections •

7. All About the SEP and SARSEP IRA _____ **119**

APPENDIX A How Taxes Affect Your Investment ___ **123**

APPENDIX B IRS Tax Forms _____ **129**

GLOSSARY _____ **133**

INDEX_____ **141**

List of Tables and Figures

Table 2.1   Advantages of Tax-Deferred Growth 16

Table 2.2   Tax-Deferred Growth Comparison 18

Table 2.3   IRA Contribution Eligibility if You ARE Covered by a Company Retirement Plan 19

Table 2.4   IRA Contribution Eligibility if You ARE NOT Covered by a Company Retirement Plan 20

Table 2.5   1998 Deductible Phase Out Limits 22

Table 2.6   Future IRA Phase Out Ranges 23

Table 2.7   Comparison of Early Withdrawal Methods 31

Table 2.8   Life Expectancy Factors 33

Table 3.1   Roth IRA Contribution Limits 47

Table 3.2   Tax-Deductible Contributions Mean Greater Annual Cash Flow 58

Table 3.3   Tax-Deductible vs. Non-Deductible Contributions 59

Table 3.4   Pre-Tax Savings Mean More Money to Invest 61

Table 3.5   Final Comparison of Pre-Tax IRA and Roth IRA 62

Table 3.6   Final Comparison of Pre-Tax IRA and Roth IRA with Marginal Tax Bracket 63

Table 3.7   Final Comparison of Pre-Tax IRA and Roth IRA Using 15 Percent Tax Rate 64

Table 3.8   Final Comparison of Pre-Tax IRA and Roth IRA Using 15 and 28 Percent Tax Rates 65

Table 3.9   Roth IRA Effective Returns 68

Table 3.10   Dollar Value of Effective Returns 68

Table 4.1   Contribution Limits for the Educational IRA 71

Table 4.2   Early vs. Late Contributions 76

Table 4.3 $500 Annual Contributions Growing at 8 percent and 12
             percent 78

Table 4.4   Effect of Fixed Account Fees on Growth of Educational IRA
             80

Table 5.1   IRA Comparison 93

Table 5.2   Convert vs. Don't Convert 102

Table 6.1   Benchmark Returns 111

Table 6.2   Top Performing Mutual Funds 112

Table 6.3   Fund Company Phone Numbers 113

Table 6.4   Discount Broker Phone Numbers 115

Figure A-1   Tax Structure Diagram A-124

Table A-1   1997 Schedule Y-1 .... A-127

Note to the Reader

This book is written for you, the Individual Investor. As investment options increase, there is a great need for information that will help you make sound decisions based on your own set of circumstances. This book provides such information.

The IRA has long been an overlooked investment opportunity for many. The addition of the Roth IRA, coupled with changes to the traditional IRA, has created a wealth building opportunity never seen before. You will not find one IRA that fits all. The investment strategy that works for your coworker may not be suitable for you.

Take time to investigate the opportunities and match them with your unique needs. The right strategy will reap huge rewards.

Chapter 1

The New IRA Will Put a Smile on your Face

Are you ready to take advantage of the new IRA? Now's the time to get started and this book has everything you need to do just that! Thanks to major legislative changes implemented in 1996 and 1997, the new IRA has something for just about everyone.

For starters, you can now contribute more money into a Spousal IRA (an IRA created for a nonworking spouse). Prior to 1997, if one spouse worked and the other didn't they could only invest a total of $2,225 across their two IRA's each year. Now a couple in this situation can contribute up to $2,000 per year into both accounts for a total of $4,000. This gives you $1,775 more to work with annually. Over a span of 20 years, this $1,775 annual contribution invested at 12 percent will add an additional $127,893 to the final value of your account.

In the past, the amount of tax-deferred contributions you could make into an IRA was limited if you or your spouse had access to a company retirement plan. The 1997 Tax Payer Relief Act changed this rule so that more people can now qualify for tax-deductible contributions even if they have access to a company retirement plan. Contributions to a spousal IRA are now tax-deductible as well even if the working spouse has access to a company retirement plan. In general, more people are now able to deduct IRA contributions from their gross income regardless of coverage by a company retirement plan. If you're curious to find out if you are now eligible for tax-deductible IRA contributions, peek ahead to Tables 2.3 and 2.4.

Several changes have also been made in the area of IRA withdrawals. No additional tax is levied on early withdrawals used to cover certain medical expenses. Penalties have been eliminated on withdrawals made for certain home purchases and educational expenses. Taxes levied on distributions that exceed a predetermined amount have been repealed. In addition, taxes on certain prohibited transactions have been increased and IRA's can now invest in certain coins and bullion.

IRA Facts

- The original IRA was created almost two decades ago.

- Today, over 125 million people are saving for retirement.

- Over half the workers, some 65 million individuals, do not have access to a company retirement plan.

- Improvements made to the IRA in 1997 have created opportunities for nearly everyone.

The most noteworthy changes that came out of 1997 legislation is the creation of two new kinds of IRA's: the Roth IRA and the Educational IRA. With a Roth IRA your contributions are taxed but the money is allowed to grow tax-free, qualified withdrawals are not taxed, and you are allowed to continue growing your account tax-free after age 70 1/2 without taking mandatory withdrawals. The Educational IRA is a wonderful way to help you save for a child's college education. Chapters 3 and 4 describe these two types of IRA's in full detail.

How Many Kinds of IRA's Are There Anyway?

The original IRA that was initiated in 1974, and since had many changes made to it, is considered the traditional IRA. In 1986, tax reform knocked the wind out of the IRA's sail by restricting tax-deductible contributions to certain income levels. This created two types of IRA: one that contains tax-deductible contributions—the **traditional, tax-deductible IRA**—and one that contains taxable contributions—the **traditional, nondeductible IRA**. Both allow you to defer paying taxes on accumulated gains until you retire. All tax-deferred money is taxed as ordinary income when distributed. This works out well if you drop to a lower tax rate when you retire. The mechanics for contributions, investments, and distribution are the same for both types of traditional IRA's. You will learn more about how the traditional IRA works in Chapter 2.

> ### History of the IRA
>
> During the 70's and early 80's, the IRA was modified by tax and revenue acts almost every year. It became a significant wealth accumulation vehicle that offered tax-deferred investing and versatility. Then came the Tax Reform Act of 1986 (TRA of 1986). With one sweeping piece of legislation, many IRA advantages were eliminated. IRA investing became unattractive and many people turned to highly marketed products such as limited partnerships and variable annuities. In time, these investors realized the mistake of these fancy investments but the IRA had become an investment vehicle that was neither understood or respected.

The 1997 Tax Payer Relief Act created two new types of IRA's. The Roth IRA and the Educational IRA. The **Roth IRA**, named after the congressman who championed it, takes a different approach to tax-deferred investing. With this type of IRA, your contributions are *not* tax-deductible. Your money, however, is allowed to grow tax-free and qualified withdrawals are tax-free as well. The Roth IRA is covered in Chapter 3.

The **Educational IRA** has some of the features of a traditional IRA and some of the features of the new Roth IRA. Although called an IRA, it is really an investment vehicle that will help you save for a child's education. Your contributions are *not* tax-deductible but the earnings may be disbursed tax-free if used for educational expenses. The Educational IRA is covered in Chapter 4.

The IRA may also be used as a retirement plan for self-employed and small businesses. **The Self Employed Pension (SEP)** and **SIMPLE IRA** are special types of IRA's associ-

New Life for the IRA
Legislative acts in 1996 and 1997 have breathed new life into the IRA. These changes are revolutionary. Many opportunities exist for you to increase the size of your investment portfolio. You can use the IRA as your basic building block for wealth accumulation or you can use it to complement your company retirement plan. In either case, it is a very good addition to almost every investor's portfolio.

ated with employer retirement plans. They have special features and allow for larger contributions per year. They are discussed in Chapter 7.

Chapter 2

All About the Traditional IRA

The Individual Retirement Account (IRA) was created to encourage people to save for retirement. It is available to everyone and has special tax advantages that make it a very popular investment. You can use it to accumulate retirement savings while you are still employed and you can transfer money from a qualified company retirement plan into one when you retire. An IRA is totally independent from the company you work for so you must initiate it yourself.

Not only is the IRA a trust arrangement created for a specific individual, it is also a type of investment vehicle—sort of a "shell"—that holds individual investments such as stocks, bonds, cash equivalents and mutual funds. Investments placed inside an IRA are allowed to grow tax-deferred. This gives you more money to work with which means that the final value of your account will be much larger than if you had to give part of it away to Uncle Same each year. Here's an example. If you invest $2,000 a year for 40 years at a rate of 10 percent and it is allowed to grow tax-deferred, your final account value will be $885,185. The same investment without tax-deferred growth will only be worth $420,440. You get an extra $464,745 in your pocket thanks to tax-deferral! See Table 2.1.

Table 2.1   Advantages of Tax-Deferred Growth

Year	IRA With Tax-Deferred Growth	After-Tax Account, Taxable Growth
1	$2,000	$2,000
2	$4,200	$4,144
3	$6,620	$6,442
4	$9,282	$8,906
5	$12,210	$11,547
10	$31,875	$27,895
15	$63,545	$51,039
20	$114,550	$83,804
25	$196,694	$130,190
30	$328,988	$195,858
40	$885,185	$420,440

This table shows investment growth based on whether or not your investment is allowed to grow tax-deferred. The first column shows a $2,000 contribution that grows tax-deferred. The second column shows a non-IRA investment that does not grow tax-deferred. This illustration assumes a 28 percent marginal tax bracket and a 10 percent per year return on your investment.

Tax-Deductible IRA vs. Non-Deductible IRA

As mentioned earlier, the traditional IRA comes in two forms: tax-deductible and nondeductible. These two IRA's are alike in every way except for how taxes are paid. With a **tax-deductible IRA** your contributions are tax-deferred. This infers three things: (1) When you contribute $2,000 from earned income into your account no taxes are paid on the money. (2) The $2,000 contribution is deducted from your gross income so you pay less in taxes that year. (3) Taxes on contributions and on investment growth are deferred, not eliminated entirely, meaning that they will eventually be paid when you make withdrawals during retirement. A **nondeductible IRA** has the following characteristics: (1) Your contributions are not tax-deductible. If you are in the 28 percent tax bracket it takes $2,778 of earned income to make a $2,000 contribution because you owe $778 in taxes. (2) The $2,000 contribution is not deducted from your gross income so you get no tax savings from the investment contribution. (3) Investment growth is still tax-deferred—you don't pay taxes until money is taken out of your account. Taxes are paid only on tax-deferred investment gains and not on contributions that were already taxed.

Let's get right to the heart of the matter and see how much money you'll end up with when these two types of IRA's are compared. Table 2.2 shows what happens when you have $2,000 of earned income to invest annually over a period of 40 years at a rate of 10 percent. If you put the money into a tax-deductible IRA you get a full $2,000 working for you each year and you end up with $885,185. If you put the $2,000 contribution into a nondeductible IRA, you really only get $1,440 into your investment each year because $560 is paid in taxes. As a result, you end up with $637,333. To show both sides of the story, if you invest your $2,000 in a non-IRA account where contributions and growth are both taxed, you only end up with $302,717 at the end of 40 years.

The tax-deductible IRA is obviously better than the nondeductible IRA. In fact, you'll soon see that the new Roth IRA is better than the nondeductible IRA as well. So why would anyone invest in the nondeductible version of an IRA? Before the birth of the Roth IRA, it may have been their only choice. Restrictions still apply as to who can invest in IRA's. Only certain income levels qualify for tax-deductible contributions into a traditional IRA and after-tax contributions into a Roth IRA.

The most you can contribute to a traditional IRA is $2,000

Table 2.2   Tax-Deferred Growth Comparison

Year	Tax-Deductible IRA Contributions and Tax-Deferred Growth	After-Tax IRA Contributions and Tax-Deferred Growth	After-Tax Account, Taxable Investment, Contributions and Growth
1	$2,000	$1,440	$1,440
2	$4,200	$3,024	$2,984
3	$6,620	$4,766	$4,639
4	$9,282	$6,683	$6,412
5	$12,210	$8,791	$8,314
10	$31,875	$22,950	$20,085
15	$63,545	$45,752	$36,748
20	$114,550	$82,476	$60,339
25	$196,694	$141,620	$93,736
30	$328,988	$236,871	$141,018
40	$885,185	$637,333	$302,717

This table shows investment growth when $2,000 of earned income is subject to different tax situations. In the first column, the $2,000 contribution is tax-deductible, plus it is allowed to grow tax-deferred. In the second column, you can see that $2,000 of earned income results in a $1,440 investment contribution because the contribution is not tax-deductible and taxes have been subtracted out. The investment in column two is allowed to grow tax-deferred. In column three, only $1,440 is available to invest and the investment does not grow tax-deferred. You can see that tax deduction and tax deferral results in a much larger account value.

per year. Depending on your income level, whether or not you have access to a company retirement plan, and your IRS filing status, you may be eligible to contribute the full $2,000 on a tax-deductible basis. It is also possible that only part of your $2,000 is eligible for tax deduction. In the worse scenario, you may not qualify for tax deductions on any amount of your $2,000 contribution (of course you can always contribute up to $2,000 a year in after-tax money). The good news is that the 1997 Tax Payer Relief Act has modified eligibility requirements so that more people can take advantage of tax-deductible contributions. You may qualify now even if you didn't before.

A full $2,000 tax-deductible contribution is allowed if you and your spouse do not have access to, or are not allowed to participate in, a company retirement plan. Starting in 1998, a full $2,000 tax-deductible contribution is available for a spouse that does not have a retirement plan even if the other spouse does. The qualifications are limited to couples whose Modified Adjusted Gross Income (MAGI—see Appendix A for definition) is under $150,000. Your $2,000 is also fully deductible if your income is within a predefined level. Table 2.3 and Table

Table 2.3   1998 IRA Contribution Eligibility if You ARE Covered By a Company Retirement Plan

If your Modified AGI is at least...	But less than...	Single or Head of Household	Married Filing Jointly	Married Filing Separately
$0.01	$10,000	Full Deduction	Full Deduction	Partial
$10,000	$30,000	Full Deduction	Full Deduction	No Deduction
$30,000	$40,000	Partial	Full Deduction	No Deduction
$40,000	$50,000	No Deduction	Full Deduction	No Deduction
$50,000	$60,000	No Deduction	Partial	No Deduction
$60,000	or over	No Deduction	No Deduction	No Deduction

Table 2.4 1998 IRA Contribution Eligibility if You ARE NOT Covered By a Company Retirement Plan

If your Modified AGI is at least...	But less than...	Single or Head of Household	Married Filing Jointly (spouse is covered by plan at work)	Married Filing Jointly (spouse is NOT covered by plan at work)	Married Filing Separately
$0.01	$10,000	Full Deduction	Full Deduction	Full Deduction	Full Deduction
$10,000	$30,000	Full Deduction	Full Deduction	Full Deduction	Full Deduction
$30,000	$40,000	Full Deduction	Full Deduction	Full Deduction	Full Deduction
$40,000	$150,000	Full Deduction	Full Deduction	Full Deduction	Full Deduction
$150,000	$160,000	Full Deduction	Partial	Full Deduction	Full Deduction
$160,000	or over	Full Deduction	No Deduction	Full Deduction	Full Deduction

2.4 show whether you qualify for a full deduction, a partial deduction, or no deduction at all. Use Table 2.3 if you are covered by a retirement plan at work. Use Table 2.4 if you aren't covered. If you qualify for a partial deduction, Table 2.5 will tell you the exact dollar value that qualifies. Tables 2.3, 2.4, and 2.5 are for 1998 only. The deductible phaseout limits are to be increased each year for the next 10 years. See Table 2.6 for a look into the future.

If you and your spouse are employed, you can both contribute up to $2,000 a year into an IRA—one IRA for you and one for your spouse. Your total contribution would then be $4,000. If only one of you is employed, you can set up a regular account and a spousal account. It used to be that a married couple with only one earned income could contribute only $2,225 across the regular IRA and the spousal IRA. Now $2,000 can be contributed into both accounts for a total of $4,000.

When you contribute to an IRA, the money must come from earned income—wages, salaries, tips, and bonuses—it cannot come from investment income. You do not have to deposit the same amount of money into your IRA each year and you can stop contributions whenever you like. Annual contributions do not have to be deposited all at once. It is possible to fund your IRA with a no-load mutual fund company for as little as $25 a month. Let's look at some examples.

Examples of Contribution Eligibility

Joe is single and earns $20,000 a year. He has a company retirement plan at work. His Modified Adjusted Gross Income (MAGI) is also $20,000. By looking at Table 2.5, you can see that Joe is eligible for a full $2,000 tax-deductible contribution to an IRA. If Joe's MAGI increases to $35,000, he will only be eligible for a $1,000 tax-deductible contribution. He can still contribute another $1,000 to his IRA but this is after-tax money. If Joe did not have a company retirement plan at work he would be eligible for the full tax-deductible contribution regardless of income level.

Table 2.5   1998 Deductible Phase-Out Limits

Single MAGI	Deductible	Married MAGI	Deductible
$30,000	$2,000	$50,000	$2,000
$30,500	$1,900	$50,500	$1,900
$31,000	$1,800	$51,000	$1,800
$31,500	$1,700	$51,500	$1,700
$32,000	$1,600	$52,000	$1,600
$32,500	$1,500	$52,500	$1,500
$33,000	$1,400	$53,000	$1,400
$33,500	$1,300	$53,500	$1,300
$34,000	$1,200	$54,000	$1,200
$34,500	$1,100	$54,500	$1,100
$35,000	$1,000	$55,000	$1,000
$35,500	$900	$55,500	$900
$36,000	$800	$56,000	$800
$36,500	$700	$56,500	$700
$37,000	$600	$57,000	$600
$37,500	$500	$57,500	$500
$38,000	$400	$58,000	$400
$38,500	$300	$58,500	$300
$39,000	$200	$59,000	$200
$39,500	$100	$59,500	$100
$40,000	$0	$60,000	$0

If you qualify for a partial deduction (see Tables 2.3 and 2.4) to a traditional, tax-deductible IRA, this table will show you the exact dollar value that qualifies. Your deductible contribution is reduced by $10 for every $50 increase in income over the full deductible MAGI amount. This table is for 1998 only. The deductible phaseout limits are to be increased each year for the next 10 years. See Table 2.6 for a look into the future.

Jenny is single, earns $60,000 a year and is eligible to participate in her company retirement plan. Her MAGI is $60,000. She is not eligible for a tax-deductible IRA contribution. She may, however, contribute up to $2,000 of after-tax money into an IRA and it will grow tax-deferred.

Rick and Joanne are married and file jointly. Rick earns $30,000 a year and has a company retirement plan. Joanne works part time earning $5,000 a year. Their combined earned income is $35,000 and their MAGI is also $35,000. Because their MAGI is less than $50,000, they are eligible for a fully tax-deductible IRA contribution. Rick and Joanne both have earned income greater than $2,000 so they are each eligible for a $2,000 tax-deductible contribution into their own IRA. This gives them a total of $4,000 in tax-deductible contributions.

Using **Rick and Joanne** again, let's look at their IRA eligibility if Joanne earns $1,000 instead of $5,000. Their total

Table 2.6   Future IRA Phase-Out Ranges

Year	Married Filing Jointly		Single Filer	
	Max salary for full deduction	Salary where deduction is phased out	Max salary for full deduction	Salary where deduction is phased out
1998	$50,000	$60,000	$30,000	$40,000
1999	$51,000	$61,000	$31,000	$41,000
2000	$52,000	$62,000	$32,000	$42,000
2001	$53,000	$63,000	$33,000	$43,000
2002	$54,000	$64,000	$34,000	$44,000
2003	$60,000	$70,000	$40,000	$40,000
2004	$65,000	$75,000	$45,000	$55,000
2005	$70,000	$80,000	$50,000	$60,000
2006	$75,000	$85,000	$50,000	$60,000
2007	$80,000	$100,000	$50,000	$60,000

earned income is now $31,000. They are still eligible for full tax-deductible contributions into an IRA. Rick may contribute $2,000 tax-deductible into his IRA but Joanne may only contribute up to $1,000 into her IRA because that's all she earned. This gives them a total of $3,000 in tax-deductible contributions. They may now contribute another $1,000 of Rick's earned income tax-deductible to Joanne's IRA under the spousal IRA rules. Now Joanne's account has the full $2,000.

Bob and Cathy are married and each earn $60,000 a year. They have a MAGI of $120,000. Neither are eligible to participate in a retirement plan so they are each entitled to make a $2,000 tax-deductible contribution into their own IRA account.

Bill and Debbie are married and file jointly. Bill earns $30,000 per year and Debbie earns $80,000. Her company has a 401(k) plan in which she is eligible to participate. Bill does not have a company retirement plan. They are married filing jointly and have a MAGI of $110,000. Since Debbie has a company retirement plan and earns more than the income limitation, she is not eligible for a tax-deductible IRA contribution. She can still make a $2,000 after-tax contribution. Bill does not have a company retirement plan. Since their combined MAGI is less than $150,000 he is eligible for the full $2,000 tax-deductible contribution.

If **Bill** from the previous example makes $65,000. He will still be eligible for a tax-deductible contribution since he does not have a retirement plan and their MAGI is $145,000 which is less than the $150,000 income limitation. If Bill makes $85,000 a year he will no longer be eligible for the tax deductible contribution because it would push their MAGI to $165,000 which is above the income limitation for spousals with an active company retirement plan.

Denise and William both make $100,000 per year. They file jointly and have a MAGI of $200,000. Neither has a company retirement plan. They both are eligible for a full tax-deductible IRA contribution. If either spouse gains access to a company retirement plan then neither of them would be able to take a tax deduction for the IRA contribution.

Taxes are only deferred. Don't forget about them!

Of course you eventually must pay taxes on your IRA money, but this doesn't happen until you retire and begin making withdrawals. By this time your tax bracket may be lower. More importantly, your account value will likely be very large due to the compounding of interest over a long period of time. The power of compounding interest allows you to build wealth using the tax-deferred money. You only pay taxes on the tax-deductible money or tax-deferred money. Any money that was contributed on an after-tax bases is not taxed when withdrawn.

The above examples illustrate several scenarios of IRA tax deductibility. Each scenario assumes that earned income is the same as Modified Adjusted Gross Income (MAGI). This is not typically the case for a variety of reasons (see Appendix A for definition of MAGI). Be sure to review your IRS 1040 form to determine your tax position. This form has worksheets that walk you through the calculations.

How to Get Money into Your IRA

There are two ways to get money into your IRA. The first is to make annual contributions up to the yearly limit of $2,000. The second way is to transfer money into your IRA from a tax-qualified retirement plan belonging to either yourself or your deceased spouse. Funds transferred or rolled over from another account are not subject to the $2,000 per year limit. Any money in the tax-qualified retirement plan that was not contributed on a tax-deferred basis may not be rolled into your IRA account. For now it's important to know that transferring funds from your company retirement plan into an IRA can give you greater control over your money because you have more flexibility and more investment options to choose from. Be sure that you know something about investing before you do this. If you get into a poor investment it may be very costly to get out of.

The IRS allows IRA contributions to be as late as the last allowable tax filing day. This is typically April 15 of the year following the current tax year. You can make a contribution for the 1998 tax year as late as April 15, 1999. Of course, the sooner you make the contributions the sooner your investment goes to work for you. Be sure your IRA statement records the proper year for your contribution.

How to Keep Track of Taxes Owed

As you know, when you contribute money to a traditional IRA it's going in either as tax-deductible money or as non-tax-deductible money. In either case, you pay taxes, it's just a matter of when. If your contribution is *not* tax-deductible, then you pay taxes on the money before it goes into your IRA. If your contribution *is* deductible, then you pay taxes when you begin drawing money out during retirement.

The only conditions under which you can make tax-deductible contributions is if you do not have access to a company retirement plan or if your income is within a predefined range (see Table 2.5). You may find yourself with an IRA that has commingled money— some of the contributions were made tax-deductible and some were not. This happens with a nondeductible IRA where contributions are taxed and investment gains are tax-deferred. This will also happen when you transfer a lump sum from your company's retirement plan into an IRA that has non tax-deductible contributions in it.

In any event, IRS form 8606 is used to keep track of non-tax-deductible contributions by recording which taxes were already paid so that you don't have to pay again when you withdraw the money. It is your responsibility to track this information. Submit form 8606 each year in which you make after-tax contributions. Maintain your records for the life of your IRA. You are subject to a fine if you fail to submit this form at the appropriate time. Don't let any of this paperwork keep you from starting a non-tax-deductible IRA if it makes sense in your portfolio. Form 8606 is easy to fill out. *A little paper work once a year is well worth the tax deferment your investment receives.*

As you make withdrawals on a commingled account, you will have a certain percentage of money that you owe taxes on. IRS Form 1099-R is used to report IRA distributions. You only pay taxes on money that was tax-deferred. The IRS has a special formula used to calculate which portion of your withdrawal was made from taxable funds. You cannot arbitrarily claim that your entire withdrawal is from money already taxed. Each withdrawal will have some percentage of taxes due. Form 8606 will remind you what taxes were already paid.

Conduit IRA

If you roll over or transfer money from your employer's qualified retirement plan into an IRA, it is better to maintain that money in a separate IRA account. This is called a *conduit IRA*. It is used as a path between past and future employer plans and it prevents you from losing tax qualifications. If you make no outside contributions to your conduit account, taxed or non-taxed, and do not commingle the funds with other IRA money, you may be able to transfer conduit IRA money to another employer's qualified plan if you choose to. This may be advantageous to some investors. There is no special name on the IRA that designates it as a conduit IRA. It is just the fact that only money rolled over from a qualified employer plan resides in it. If you don't want to transfer your IRA to a future employer's qualified plan, a conduit IRA is not needed. You can continue making contributions into a conduit IRA following the same guidelines as a regular IRA. When you create an IRA for the purpose of a conduit, let your IRA trustee know so that your intentions will remain clear. This will help your future retirement plan trustee to accept your IRA rollover.

IRA Distributions

IRA's are designed to save for retirement. If you withdraw money prior to age 59 1/2 you will be subject to penalties. You can also expect to pay penalties if you fail to make mandatory withdrawals after age 70 1/2 (this is not the case with a Roth IRA). There is, however, a way to start distributions from your IRA prior to age 59 1/2 without paying penalties. Let's take a look at this and then see what kind of distributions you can make between age 59 1/2 and 70 1/2 and then age 70 1/2 and older.

Distributions Before Age 59 1/2

If you are under age 59 1/2 and make an IRA withdrawal, you must pay current income taxes and a 10 percent early withdrawal penalty. You can avoid the 10 percent penalty, but not ordinary taxes, if the money withdrawn is used for qualified, higher educational expenses, for first-time homebuyer expenses, or if you make the withdrawal according to the conditions outlined by what is called *substantially equal distributions*.

Qualified, higher educational expenses, as defined by the 1997 Taxpayer Relief Act, include books, tuition, fees, supplies and any equipment required for enrollment or attendance at an eligible educational institution. Any college, university, vocational school, or other post secondary educational institution that is eligible to participate in the student aid programs administered by the Department of Education are considered eligible for this purpose. Room and board expenses are also considered qualified expenses if the student is enrolled at least halftime in an eligible institution.

The amount of money that you can withdraw from your IRA penalty-free to pay for educational expenses is reduced by any scholarships or educational assistance you may receive. It is also reduced by tax-free distributions from an Educational IRA. You can use the early IRA withdrawal to pay for educational expenses for you, your spouse, your children or your grandchildren.

The 1997 Tax Payer Relief Act also allows you to avoid the 10 percent early withdrawal penalty if the money is used for first-time homebuyer expenses. You are considered a first-time home buyer if you had no ownership interest in a principle residence during the 2 year period ending on the date you acquire a house to be used as your principle residence. The maximum amount of money you can withdraw from your IRA over the course of your lifetime for this purpose is $10,000. The money can be used for any qualified family member—you, your spouse, your children, your grandchildren, your parents or any other ancestor. The first-time homebuyer qualification applies to the person or couple buying, building or remodeling. In other words, if you do not qualify as first-time homebuyer but your child does, you are still exempt from paying the 10 percent penalty if the money goes toward the child's expenses. In any event, the distribution must be made 120 days before the primary residence is purchased, built or remodeled.

> ### First-Time Home Buyer
>
> A first-time home buyer does not mean you have never owned a home. It is defined as not owning a home in the last two years!

Denise and William withdraw $4,000 to purchase their first home. This withdrawal is penalty-free. Three years later they sell the home and rent a house. After two years they decide to purchase another home. They are once again considered first-time buyers because they did not own a principle residence in the previous two years. They may withdraw up to $6,000 ($10,000 lifetime less $4,000 previous) from their IRA to purchase this home.

The IRS also realizes that some individuals will retire early. Another way you can avoid the 10 percent early withdrawal penalty is if you take what is known as *substantially equal distributions* for at least five years or until you reach age 59 1/2 whichever method covers a longer period of time. Substantially equal does not mean that each of your distributions are exactly the same amount. It means that each withdrawal is based on the same set of conditions, but the conditions change each year. For example, both your life expectancy and your account value change from year-to-year. You may also amortize your account based on interest rate assumptions.

There are two ways to calculate your substantially equal distribution payouts. The first is called the *life expectancy method*. The second is called the *amortization method*.

The **life expectancy method** is easy to calculate but provides the smallest annual payment. It is the same method as the *minimum withdrawal calculation* used to calculate the amount of money you must withdraw from your IRA when you reach age 70 1/2. You will see an example of this calculation shortly. The difference between the two methods is that the minimum withdrawal calculation determines the minimum amount you must take out of your IRA when you hit age 70 1/2. The life expectancy method calculates the exact amount you are allowed to withdraw from an IRA prior to age 59 1/2.

The **amortization method** amortizes your account based on both life expectancy and an assumed interest rate. It takes into account the growth of your investment with respect to the interest it is earning. The amortization is much like your home mortgage. Calculations require use of IRS actuary tables for life expectancy. The assumed interest rate must be reasonable. This method will provide a larger payout than the life expectancy method.

If you choose to use the amortization method for calculating withdrawals, I recommend you enlist the help of a qualified tax professional.

Table 2.7 shows what your distribution would be using the two distribution methods. As you can see, there is a big difference in how much you can withdraw depending on which method you choose. Remember that if you start an early retirement distribution prior to age 59 1/2 you must continue that distribution for at least 5 years, or until you are 59 1/2, whichever is longer. If you don't, the prior distributions will be considered a withdrawal and you will have to pay the 10 percent penalty. You can start IRA distributions using the substantially equal method at any age—you don't actually have to be retired. Since the IRA is meant for retirement, it doesn't make sense to start withdrawals unless you really need the money.

Table 2.7 Comparison of Early Withdrawal Methods

Age	IRS Joint Life Expectancy	Life Expectancy Method	Amorization Method
57	32.5	$3,077	$9,095
58	31.5	$3,323	$9,095
59	30.5	$3,589	$9,095
60	29.5	$3,876	$9,095
61	28.5	$4,186	$9,095

This chart shows the difference in annual withdrawal amounts calculated using the two different withdrawal methods. Use this comparison to determine which method is best for you.

Distributions Between Age 59 1/2 and 70 1/2

If you are in this age group you have the most flexibility when it comes to IRA withdrawals. You can allow the money to continue growing tax-deferred until you reach age 70 1/2 or you can make withdrawals of any amount you desire. It may be necessary to continue making minimum withdrawals if you started your withdrawals prior to age 59 1/2.

You can continue to contribute to your IRA as long as you have earned income. Once you reach 70 1/2 years of age you must stop making contributions and you must begin to make minimum withdrawals.

Distributions at Age 70 1/2 and Older

Up until age 70 1/2, the IRS allowed you to accumulate your IRA savings tax-deferred but by this age they want the tax revenue back. You must begin making mandatory withdrawals beginning in the year you turn 70 1/2 years of age (this is not required with the Roth IRA). The first distribution must be made by April 1 of the year after you turn 70 1/2 and you must continue distributions each year. If you turn 70 1/2 in 1998, you must make your first distribution by April 1 1999. You must also make your second distribution by December 31 1999.

If you do not make the minimum withdrawal you will be taxed 50 percent of the amount that was not withdrawn. For example, if your minimum withdrawal is $1,000 and you only take out $900, then $100 of your account will be taxed at 50 percent. You can always withdraw more than the minimum amount. As mentioned earlier, minimum withdrawals are calculated using the **life expectancy method**. The amount of your minimum withdrawals will vary each year because your account value will be different at the beginning of each year and your life expectancy decreases each year. This is what we referred to earlier as *substantially equal payments*.

It's easy to calculate minimum distributions using the life expectancy method. Just divide your account balance at the beginning of the year by the number of years in your life expectancy. Your account balance is the valuation of your account as of December 31 for the prior year. For example, when calculating your minimum withdrawal for 1998 use the valuation of your account as of December 31, 1997.

There are two different ways to calculate your life expectancy. The first method uses life expectancy tables to determine your new life expectancy each year based on your new age. The second method uses a constant declining life expectancy calculation by subtracting one year off your original life expectancy age when you started taking minimum withdrawals. Table 2.8 shows what your single life expectancy is using the two different methods. Once you choose a method, you must stick with it for the remaining years.

You can use joint life expectancy numbers. This is useful if your beneficiary is your spouse because it helps prevent depleting your account prior to the life expectancy of the younger spouse. Using the joint life expectancy numbers will reduce your required minimum withdrawal since your joint life expectancy is longer. Let's look at an example.

Bill has an IRA valued at $100,000 on December 31, 1997. He turns 70 1/2 years of age in March of 1998. His birthday is in September when he turns 71. His wife is the sole beneficiary and she turns 65 on her birthday during 1998. What is the minimum distribution that must be taken by Bill from his IRA?

Bill decides to use the joint life expectancy method to calculate his IRA distributions. Since Bill turned 71 in 1998 he uses this age to determine his life expectancy. Bill's wife turned 65 in 1998 so he uses 65 to calculate her life expectancy. From the

Table 2.8 Single Life Expectancy Factors

Age	Constant	Variable
70	16	16
71	15	15.3
72	14	14.6
73	13	13.9
74	12	13.2
75	11	12.5
76	10	11.9
77	9	11.2
78	8	10.6
79	7	10
80	6	9.5
81	5	8.9
82	4	8.4
83	3	7.9
84	2	7.4
85	1	6.9

This table contains single life expectancy factors used for calculating minimum distributions for single life.
Source: IRS Publication 939 (Jan 90)

IRS joint life expectancy tables for ages 71 and 65 the joint life expectancy in years is 22.8. This will be the divisor for calculating the first minimum withdrawal. Use the following formula for calculating Bill's minimum withdrawal for 1998:

minimum withdrawal = account value / life expectancy

= $100,000 / 22.8

= $4,385.96

Bill must withdraw $4,385.96 by April 1, 1999. This is his 1998 withdrawal. His next withdrawal must occur by December 31, 1999. This would be Bill's 1999 withdrawal. Assuming Bill's account makes zero gains, calculate his minimum withdrawal for 1999.

By December 1998, Bill's account value has dropped by $4,385.96 due to his initial withdrawal. In other words, his account value on December 31, 1998 was

$100,000 - $4,385.96 = $95,614.04.

Since Bill selected the constant life expectancy calculation he subtracts one from the joint life value of 22.8 determined in 1998. Life expectancy for 1999 withdrawal calculation is

22.8 -1 = 21.8.

minimum withdrawal = account value / life expectancy

= $95,614.04 / 21.8

= $4,385.96

If Bill waits until April 1, 1999 to make his first withdrawal, he will end up making two withdrawals that year because his second withdrawal is due by December 31, 1999. This could create a tax problem because he is taking two distributions in one year.

If your beneficiary is not your spouse there are certain rules that apply to the calculation of joint beneficiaries. If the named beneficiary is more than 10 years younger than you, you must adjust his / her age to within 10 years of yours when calculating a joint beneficiary. This prevents you from naming a person who is 40 years younger in order to reduce the minimum withdrawals you are required to make.

Penalties for Excessive Withdrawals

In the past, withdrawals above a certain level where considered excessive and subject to a 15 percent penalty. The 1996 minimum wage bill enacted a provision which suspended the excessive withdrawal penalty for three years. The 1997 Tax Payer Relief Act repealed the excessive penalty provision. At this time there is no penalty for accumulating a large portfolio and withdrawing large sums during retirement!

Rollovers and Transfers

You can transfer your IRA to another investment organization whenever you want. This gives you the opportunity to choose from investments that may not have been available previously. There are two ways to transfer your IRA to another IRA, the *direct transfer* and the *rollover* from IRA to IRA.

With a **direct transfer**, your IRA money is transferred directly from your current agent to the new agent. It is easy to initiate this transaction. The agents will handle all the details for you. You can transfer your money in this fashion tax free as many times as you like.

The second method of transferring your money from one IRA to another is the **rollover**. This method can only be used once a year. With an IRA rollover, the agent sends your money directly to you. You have access to the money for 60 days at which time you must deposit the money into another qualified plan. If you fail to do this, the money is considered a withdrawal and subject to ordinary income taxes and perhaps even an early withdrawal penalty. The same property withdrawn (stocks, bonds, cash) must be placed in the new IRA. Typically, the withdrawal for a rollover will be cash. The rollover we are discussing here only applies to IRA rollovers. A lump sum distribution from your company retirement plan does not get the full benefit of the 60 day rule.

TIP: It is recommended that you use the direct agent transfer method to move your money from one IRA to another. It provides a seamless transfer when changing investment managers.

Some people use the IRA rollover to get working capital for 60 days. This can be dangerous. If you fail to get the money into another qualified plan within 60 days you will have to pay ordinary income taxes and a 10 percent penalty. You may also miss out on investment growth by being out of the market.

Estate Planning

An IRA is a trust set up for the sole benefit of the person who owns it. There is no such thing as a joint account even for married couples. An IRA does allow you to designate a beneficiary. If your beneficiary is a person, as opposed to an estate, than the proceeds of your IRA avoid probate. If your IRA beneficiary is your estate, then your account will go thorough probate and will be subjected to all related probate taxes and fees.

The most powerful estate planning feature the IRA offers is the spousal beneficiary. If your spouse is your beneficiary, then this person may roll your IRA into his / her IRA, avoid probate and continue tax deferment. This avoids ordinary income taxes. If your spouse chooses not to continue deferment, he / she can pay ordinary income taxes and use the money without subject to penalty.

If you choose someone other than your spouse as your beneficiary, then this person is responsible for current income taxes on the money. The beneficiary may choose to take the benefit over a five year period or to take it as a lump sum. If you name three children as beneficiaries, they can each choose a different method of distribution. Some quirks are involved if your beneficiary is used to calculate your joint life expectancy and you reached 70 1/2 and started distributions. See your tax advisor about this situation.

There is never an early or excessive withdrawal penalty applied to an IRA distribution when the distribution is made due to death.

Investments Allowed In An IRA

IRA's allow for a wide range of investment choices but some investments are not allowed. For example, you cannot purchase collectibles, life insurance or your own personal property via an IRA. You can purchase just about any type of security you'd like. Examples include stocks, bonds and cash equivalents. These investments can be in the form of individual securities, mutual funds or some other type of pooled investment fund. You may even purchase bullion and certain coins. Beginning in 1998 you can invest in certain platinum coins, gold, silver, and platinum bullion. These investments will not be considered collectibles if the platinum coins are minted and issued by the Treasury Department and the bullion meets or exceeds the minimum fineness standard. Keep in mind that just because an investment can be purchased via an IRA does not mean it is a good or suitable investment for you. You can lose money inside an IRA just as easily as outside the IRA.

You should not purchase tax-exempt or tax-deferred investments inside your IRA because your IRA is already a tax-deferred vehicle. If you purchase tax-exempt bonds inside your IRA you will still pay taxes on the tax exempt interest when you take distributions. You have therefore received a lower return on the tax exempt securities and will pay unnecessary taxes when you take distributions. Likewise, do not set up your IRA as a variable annuity. The annuity contract adds no value to your investment tax deferral or gain and will burden you with unnecessary hidden charges. The IRA already provides a better tax deferment than a variable annuity.

Tax deferral of an IRA works best when growth investments are selected. The best opportunity is usually with growth stocks and high quality bonds. Your asset selection will vary depending on your age, investment strategy and risk tolerance. Chapter 6 will take a closer look at IRA investment opportunities.

How to Start An IRA

An IRA is very easy to set up and use. It can be arranged through a brokerage house, bank, savings and loan, credit union, mutual fund group or any other qualified agent. You need only complete some simple paper work that has to do with a custodial or trust agreement. Most trustees use a form that is derived from the IRA prototype form 5305. The agent that administers your account will keep track of the contributions you make and supply you with a statement at the end of the year.

It is your responsibility to make sure you do not exceed $2,000 total in contributions per year. You must also keep track of which portion of your contribution is deductible and nondeductible as was discussed earlier in the chapter. It is also your responsibility to start and maintain minimum withdrawals when the time comes. You may want to consult a tax specialist if you are unsure about your responsibilities.

In most cases, you will want your IRA to be set up as self-directed. This means that you get to choose which investments you want your IRA savings invested in. Any investments placed in your IRA must have your approval. The self-directed IRA gives you the most freedom, however your investment choices are limited to the products available through the organization where you established your IRA account.

Most **banks** and **credit unions** will open an IRA account for you, but your investment choices may be limited to certificates of deposits, or savings accounts. These are poor investments for an IRA because the rate of return is very low. Many banks are starting to sell mutual funds and are beginning to offer more choices, but you will be limited to their product lines.

Insurance companies can administer IRA accounts. Your money typically goes into an individual retirement annuity that is either fixed or variable. Insurance company annuities are usually expensive and your investment options are limited. It is *not* a good wealth building strategy to set up an IRA with an insurance company. The IRA already offers tax deferral. The cost of the insurance product when set up as an IRA adds no value to your investment vehicle. If you do decide to set up your IRA account with an insurance company, look closely at the fees. They are often hidden.

Brokerage houses offer the widest variety of investment choices. You can choose either a full service or discount broker. Full service brokers charge more for transactions and service fees. They may also be inclined to steer you into their own products or products with high commissions. All full service brokerage products will come with one or some combination of a front-end, back-end, or continual sales load. Discount brokers do not offer investment advice. In exchange, you are charged lower

> A good investment strategy that includes an IRA can improve the success of your long-term goals.

transaction fees. There will be account representatives to help you get information and answer questions about investments. The discount brokers are experiencing competitive pricing. Every discount broker is cutting fees and adding services. You will see account and transaction fees waived. There are also low-load and no-load mutual fund services, plus better investment research services. Charles Schwab, Jake White, Waterhouse and Fidelity all offer no transaction fee networks of mutual funds. Many of the mutual funds are no-load. Some of the best no-load fund families with access to top mutual funds can be found within these networks. But be careful. Networks also contain sales-loaded funds and funds with transaction fees.

There are many low and no-load **mutual funds** that will set up your IRA directly. You will usually have several mutual funds to choose from within the same fund family. Account fees are typically inexpensive and run about $10 per fund. Many funds will waive account fees if your account is over a certain value. You should be able to find a top performing fund that doesn't have sales loads or hidden fees. There are several excellent no-load fund families to choose from. They come complete with IRA account set up, automatic deposit and withdrawals systems, low initial investments and telephone services. If you don't like the fund family you are with you can do a direct transfer of some or all your money to another fund family. Working directly with no-load mutual fund groups is a very popular (and profitable) way to set up your IRA. Some mutual fund groups allow you to make automatic direct deposits of as little as $25 per month from your bank account into your IRA. This is a powerful way to accumulate wealth.

How Many IRA's Can You Have?

There is no limit to the number of IRA's you may have. You are only limited to the amount of money you can contribute each year. If you have three separate IRA's, you are still limited to a total contribution of $2,000 for any year.

The IRA is an important retirement investment vehicle. It serves as a primary source for individuals who do not have a company retirement plan. It is also a good secondary retirement investment for those who do. You can have as many IRA's as you want. You are only limited by the yearly contribution of $2,000.

In the next few years it will most likely be common for individuals to have several IRA accounts. For example, one account can be set up as a conduit to hold money from a company contribution plan. A second account can be used for non-tax-deductible contributions. And a third can be used for tax-deductible contributions. You may even use several IRA's in order to take advantage of different investment opportunities. You may have an IRA set up with two or three different no-load funds. This will allow you to take advantage of the best funds available by spreading your money among different fund families. All IRA's held by an individual are treated as one large IRA for distribution purposes. You do not have to take equal portions out of each individual IRA.

There is a down side of having more then one IRA. Almost every administrator charges an annual fee to set up and maintain an IRA account. It runs from about $10 for many no-load mutual fund groups up to $75 or more for brokerage firms, banks and Insurance companies. Unless you have accumulated a large some of money, having too many IRA's will decrease the return yield. When you pay high fees you reduce the amount of money you keep. On a good note, many no-load mutual funds waive the annual fee if your account is above a certain value. This level is typically $5,000.

The new trend with discount brokers is to set up a no transaction fee network of various no-load funds. This will allow you to have one account in which you can access some of the best mutual funds that exist. This makes it convenient to consolidate your statements.

Chapter 3

All About the Roth IRA

The Roth IRA is a new creation. It is radically different from the traditional IRA. Whenever a new investment vehicle is created, accompanying legislation tends to be poorly worded—leaving gray areas and omissions. Unintended loop holes are often discovered after the law is enacted. The Roth IRA is no exception. As the information in this book is being prepared, congress is reviewing several areas for technical corrections. Legislation is being interpreted as Roth IRA investment products are being created. In reality, we are faced with the intent of congress, the actual wording of legislation, IRS interpretation, and the interpretation of the investment world which includes us as individuals.

Over the next year we will likely see a tax corrections bill, IRS interpretive bulletins, IRS publications with their interpretations, private letter rulings, and eventually a tax court case. The production of this book was timed to get a good feel for both the IRS interpretations and the tax correction bill. As this book goes to print, a tax correction bill has been passed by the house, but the senate has a vastly different version and the final outcome has not been resolved. It may be prudent to wait until late in 1998 to see how the interpretations turns out if you plan to use some of the gray areas. Don't wait until every wrinkle has been ironed out to include the Roth IRA in your portfolio if it makes sense in your situation. You won't run into any problems if you follow the basic intent of the program. Some opportunities associated with the Roth IRA will be lost after 1998.

An explanation of pending tax correction items and possible problems is addressed toward the end of this chapter but let's first take a good look at the intent of the IRA. It is certainly an investment opportunity worth looking into.

How the Plan Works

For years the question has been pondered whether it is better to pay taxes associated with retirement investments now or to pay them later. Deferring them until later is almost always the better choice because that extra bit of money you hold onto up front will grow significantly over the years—thanks to compound interest. In the end, you will have a much larger portfolio that will produce enough cash flow to cover taxes and still provide a good after-tax return.

The Roth IRA introduces a new twist into the question. Is it better to pay *some* taxes now and *none* later? This is exactly what the Roth IRA allows you to do. Taxes are paid on contributions—but earnings are allowed to accumulate tax-free when qualified withdrawals are made.

The Roth IRA may seem straightforward but it has an incredible hidden advantage. The contributions you make become very small in comparison to the overall value of your IRA as your investment grows. In other words, your overall earnings become bigger than your year-to-year contributions. Since you are paying taxes on contributions, not growth, you are actually paying taxes on the smaller portion of your investment and not on its entire value!

That's right. You only pay taxes on a portion of your investment. This is radically different from the traditional IRA. It is not a mistake. Congressman Roth knew exactly what he was doing. Whether or not the other members knew what was going on, I don't know! With this in mind let's see how the Roth IRA works and then look at some scenario's that will help determine whether the Roth IRA is a better choice for different situations.

Basic Features of Roth IRA

- Your contributions are *not* tax-deductible.

- Investment gains are tax-free if qualified withdrawals are made.

- Minimum withdrawals are not required when you turn 70 1/2.

- Contributions can continue after age 70 1/2.

- Distributions must be made at death.

- Your Roth IRA must be kept separate from other IRA's.

- Rollovers are allowed from one Roth IRA to another Roth IRA.

- Traditional IRA's may be converted to Roth IRA's if the tax on the taxable distribution is paid.

- Contributions are limited to $2,000 per year.

- The aggregate of your contributions to Roth and non-Roth IRA's (not including the Educational IRA) cannot exceed $2,000.

- Income phaseout limitations for contributions start at $150,000 for married filers and $95,000 for single.

- Qualified withdrawals are not reported as ordinary income and will not affect your Adjusted Gross Income (AGI).

Are You Eligible?

The maximum Roth IRA contribution is $2,000 per year, but again, your contribution is *not* tax-deductible. You are only entitled to the full $2,000 annual contribution if you are a married, joint filer with a Modified Adjusted Gross Income of $150,000 or less *or* if you are a single filer with a modified adjusted gross income of $95,000 or less. The amount you can contribute is gradually phased out to zero for married, joint filers with incomes greater than $160,000 and for single filers with incomes greater than $110,000. See Table 3.1 for a table of income limitations.

If your income does not allow you to make tax-deductible contributions to a traditional IRA, you may be able to contribute to a Roth IRA. Of course you can always make taxable contributions to a traditional IRA. The Roth IRA allows contributions to continue after age 70 1/2.

Contributions to a Roth IRA, like a traditional IRA, must come from earned income. This is defined as wage, tips, salary, commission, and bonuses. It does not include investment income.

A spousal contribution may be made up to $2,000 for a nonworking (earned income) spouse. A married couple with one working spouse may contribute $2,000 per spouse for a total of $4,000 a year into IRA's.

Remember that the aggregate of contributions to Roth and non-Roth IRA's (not including the Educational IRA) cannot exceed $2,000. If you contribute $1,000 into a traditional IRA, you can only contribute a maximum of $1,000 into a Roth IRA even if you are eligible for the full $2,000 contribution.

Examples of Eligibility

Joe is single and has a Modified Adjusted Gross Income (MAGI) of $20,000. He is eligible to make a $2,000 annual contribution across the three types of IRA's (traditional, tax-deductible IRA; traditional, nondeductible IRA; and the Roth IRA) in any combination he chooses. In the first year, Joe decides to put $1,000 into a traditional, deductible IRA and to put $1,000 into a Roth. The next year he contributes all $2,000 into a traditional deductible IRA and is therefore not eligible to put anything into the Roth for that year.

Margo and Matt are married and have a MAGI of $120,000 per year. Margo is the only person with earned income. She has a company retirement plan at work. Matt

Table 3.1 Roth IRA Contribution Limits

Single Filer	Maximum Contribution	Married Filer	Maximum Contribution
$95,000	$2,000	$150,000	$2,000
$96,000	$1,860	$151,000	$1,800
$97,000	$1,730	$152,000	$1,600
$98,000	$1,600	$153,000	$1,400
$99,000	$1,460	$154,000	$1,200
$100,000	$1,330	$155,000	$1,000
$101,000	$1,200	$156,000	$800
$102,000	$1,060	$157,000	$600
$103,000	$930	$158,000	$400
$104,000	$800	$159,000	$200
$105,000	$660	$160,000	$0
$106,000	$530		
$107,000	$400		
$108,000	$260		
$109,000	$200		
$110,000	$0		

This table shows the dollar value of contributions you can make to a Roth IRA based on your salary. For single filers, the dollar amount is decreased $13.30 for every $100 increase in salary. For married filers, the dollar amount is decreased $20 for every $100 increase in salary. All results must be rounded to the lowest multiple of $10. Any result below $200 and greater then zero is allowed a $200 contribution.

does not have any income and he does not have a company retirement plan. Margo is eligible for both Roth and traditional, nondeductible IRA contributions. A spousal IRA may be established for Matt. He is eligible for a Roth, a traditional, nondeductible IRA, and a traditional, deductible IRA since he does not have a company retirement plan and their MAGI is less than $150,000. Margo invests $2,000 in a Roth IRA for herself and they establish a traditional, deductible IRA for Matt in which $2,000 is contributed. This gives them a total of $4,000 contributed into IRA's.

Sally is single and has an MAGI of $75,000. She also has a company retirement plan in which she participates. Sally is not eligible for a traditional, deductible IRA contribution because of her salary level. She may, however, make a nondeductible, traditional IRA contribution or she may make a full contribution to a Roth IRA since her AGI is less than $95,000. Once again, Sally's total IRA contribution cannot exceed the $2,000 limit.

If Sally's income increased above $95,000 she would not be eligible for the full $2,000 Roth IRA contribution. She can make a partial contribution to the Roth as long as her MAGI is less than $110,000. The difference between the $2,000 contribution limit and the amount she is eligible and makes to a Roth may be placed in a nondeductible traditional IRA. She may make contributions to two different IRA's as long as she remains under the $2,000 per year contribution limit.

Distributions

Qualified distributions of investment gains from a Roth IRA are tax-free. There are three cases when a distribution is considered qualified: (1) The withdrawal is made when you are 59 1/2 years or older. (2) The withdrawal is used for a qualified, first-time purchase of a house or for an educational expense. (3) The withdrawal is made when you suffer disability or death. In all three of these cases, your Roth IRA must be at least five years old before qualified withdrawals can be made. Withdrawals that are not qualified are subject to tax and may be subject to a *10 percent penalty.*

The Roth IRA uses a First In First Out (FIFO) method for determining if withdrawals come from contributions or if they come from investment gains. Contributions are after-tax and investment gains are pre-tax. Contributions are considered to be withdrawn first. Investment gains are not withdrawn until all contributions are withdrawn. This is different from the traditional, nondeductible IRA in which a portion of each withdrawal is from contributions and a portion of each withdrawal is from investment gains.

The Roth IRA does not require minimum distributions at age 70 1/2. You may allow your Roth IRA to grow tax-deferred until death and you can continue to make contributions after age 70 1/2. Distributions must, however, be made at death. The ability to continue tax-free growth without mandatory distributions after age 70 1/2 is a very powerful investment opportunity. It is probably the best feature of the Roth IRA and can be used as the focal point for deciding to select or convert to a Roth IRA.

Rollovers

You can roll over one Roth IRA to another, but the rollover must occur within 60 days and the same property must be placed in the new Roth

---

Roth IRA Powerful Feature

The ability to continue tax-free growth without mandatory distributions after age 70 1/2 is a very powerful investment opportunity. It is probably the best feature of the Roth IRA and can be used as the focal point for deciding to select or convert to a Roth IRA.

IRA. A rollover can occur only once per year. An agent-to-agent transfer is allowed and there is no limit on how often it is used. This is the best method used for changing investment management companies.

A traditional IRA may be rolled into a Roth IRA by means of a conversion. You may not roll over a 401(k) or other company, pre-tax investment into a Roth IRA. You may, however, roll over your company, pre-tax retirement account into a traditional IRA and then convert the traditional IRA into a Roth IRA.

Converting an IRA to a Roth IRA

As mentioned earlier, a traditional IRA may be converted into a Roth IRA by means of a conversion. To qualify, you must have a Modified Adjusted Gross Income (MAGI) of less than $100,000 in the year the conversion takes place. Do not include the taxable amount of your IRA in gross income when calculating your MAGI for conversion eligibility. Married, filing separately, returns are not eligible for conversion.

The conversion is actually a withdrawal from a traditional IRA. This causes the withdrawn funds to be included in gross income and income tax to be due. A $100,000 conversion will require $28,000 in tax payments for a person in the 28 percent tax bracket. This is a sizable amount of money to come up with. Be careful not to sacrifice investment momentum by robbing funds from existing IRA's or by using future contributions to fund the conversion. If the funds are placed in a Roth IRA within 60 days a conversion is considered to have taken place and a 10 percent penalty is not incurred.

All or part of a traditional IRA may be converted into a Roth IRA. The entire amount withdrawn must be placed into a Roth IRA within 60 days to avoid a 10 percent penalty. The same property withdrawn from the traditional IRA must be rolled into the Roth IRA. The taxable amount of the money converted into a Roth IRA is included in your gross income.

Example: Joe has a MAGI of $60,000. He has a traditional, tax-deductible, IRA containing $20,000. The entire amount is tax-deferred. Joe decides to convert his traditional IRA into a Roth IRA. Since his MAGI is less than $100,000, he is eligible for the conversion. Joe withdraws the entire $20,000 and places it into a Roth IRA within 60 days. The rollover was performed properly so he is not subject to a 10 percent penalty. Joe must now include the $20,000 withdrawal as income for the year in which the conversion occurred. Because he is in the 28 percent tax bracket, Joe should expect to pay an additional $5,600 in taxes as a result of the conversion.

If Joe had not deposited the funds into the Roth IRA within 60 days he would be subject to the additional 10 percent tax. He would owe another $2,000 for a total of $7,600.

The general rule for Roth IRA's requires that the taxable amount be included as income in the year the conversion is made. A special rule is in place for conversions made in 1999. The taxable portion must be included in gross income equally over four years. This gives investors four years to pay taxes on the conversion. This may keep your taxable income within the same marginal tax bracket!

IRS form 1099-R is used to report conversion amounts. Instructions for 1998 conversions require you to include one-fourth of the taxable amount in your income each year for four years (1998-2001). Use IRS form 8606 to determine the taxable amount for IRA's that have taxable and nontaxable funds.

Example: In the previous example, Joe moved $20,000 from a traditional, tax-deductible IRA into a Roth IRA. Even though the entire $20,000 was withdrawn in 1998, Joe must spread the taxable income equally over four years. In other words, he must claim $5,000 per year (1998, 1999, 2000, 2001) as additional income and pay an extra $1,400 in taxes in each of those four years.

The four-year tax spread is required for conversions made in 1998. Conversions made after 1998 require taxes due to be paid in full the year of the conversion. If you are considering a conversion, it may be beneficial to perform it in 1998. You can manage taxes owed each year as the result of an IRA conversion by paying taxes over a four-year period. The benefit is that the five-year period is started immediately.

A traditional IRA may be converted into a Roth IRA without actually moving your funds. You can do this by having your administrator change the trust agreement to a Roth

IRA. Of course you must still pay taxes due as required by the conversion. The benefit of this method is that you do not have to actually move your funds—you're just changing the type of IRA you have.

TIP: IRA guidance encourages trustees to hold different tax year conversions in separate Roth IRA accounts in order to simplify the identification of fund distributions. This is due to the five year holding period for qualified distributions. Most mutual fund companies are setting up conversion IRA's separate from contribution IRA's.

Estate Planning

Since the Roth IRA is a tax-free investment, distributions made to beneficiaries at death are not subject to ordinary income taxes. This is a very powerful estate planning feature. You may remember that minimum distributions are not required from a Roth IRA after age 70 1/2. This means that you can still change beneficiaries after reaching age 70 1/2. The Roth IRA will typically be considered part of the decedent's gross estate for federal estate tax purposes.

The Roth IRA eliminates many of the problems associated with the traditional IRA in terms of methods of withdrawals and types of distributions a beneficiary may take. If you plan to pass money to your beneficiaries, the Roth IRA is an excellent opportunity. Be sure, of course, to name your beneficiary.

Tax Corrections Bill

Several areas of concern regarding the Roth IRA are to be addressed in a technical corrections bill including, what the consequences are if an investor converts to a Roth IRA and later finds out that his or her AGI exceeded the $100,000 criteria; how to handle penalties associated with withdrawals from a Roth IRA prior to the five-year holding period; and tax liabilities if an investor dies prior to paying the four-year tax spread from a conversion. Other issues include closing potential loopholes concerning contributions and withdrawals.

There are two powerful proposals in the senate version that differ from current IRS interpretations. The first proposal allows investors to choose either the four-year spread or full tax payment for Roth conversions in 1998. The second proposal requires only one holding period for both contributions and all conversions into a Roth IRA. Right now separate Roth IRA's are established for contributions and conversions. Requiring only one holding period will solve a lot of problems with the Roth IRA.

Do State Taxes Apply?

Some states may try to collect income tax on Roth IRA distributions and on Roth conversions. State taxing agencies will likely exploit this area as the amount of money inside Roth IRA's grow. Even as this book is being written, state taxing agencies are trying to lay claim to distributions from employee 401(k) plans even when the individual no longer lives in that state. Fortunately, however, several states are enacting legislation that will recognize the Roth as a tax free vehicle.

If you live in a state that has income tax provisions find out if the state taxing authorities will levy taxes on your converted funds. Remember that the conversion of funds from a traditional IRA to a Roth IRA are included in gross income so you may be subject to state income taxes. At this time it looks like several income taxing states will not tax conversions. They all may decide not to. Be sure to look into this area before making a large conversion.

Most states have legislation that protects an individual's IRA from bankruptcy and sometimes other law suits. Some states, however, are claiming that this protection may not have the correct wording to automatically protect the Roth IRA. It is expected that this technical error will be corrected wherever it exists. You may want to verify what type of protection is offered in your state to see if technical corrections are needed.

How to Start a Roth IRA

The Roth IRA is set up similar to the traditional IRA—just make sure that the trust agreement is created for a Roth IRA. The paper work is quick. The IRS has already created a prototype agreement, form 5035-R, that most trustees will use or follow. It is a derivative of the traditional IRA prototype form 5305. The trustee will provide the form for you. In most cases, you will be able to set up and invest in a Roth IRA anywhere a traditional IRA is offered. Keep in mind that it is your responsibility not to exceed the $2,000 annual contribution limit. The trustee is not responsible for determining if your total IRA contributions exceed the limit or if you are eligible to make the contribution. Of course it is also your responsibility to select and monitor your IRA investment.

Investment Opportunities

The decision of whether or not to include a Roth IRA in your portfolio is anything but black and white. It may or may not be an appropriate investment opportunity for you. If you do not intend to depend heavily on your IRA during retirement (i.e. you expect to have money coming from other investments such as a pension or 401(k) plan), than the Roth IRA may be a good idea. Remember that you do not have to take minimum withdrawals at age 70 1/2 so your Roth account can continue to grow as you draw income from other investments. This is a particularly good way to offset inflation as it erodes your pension and annuity investments. As these investments decrease in value, your Roth IRA has the potential to increase in value because it is still fully invested—and it still grows tax-free!

Adding a Roth IRA to your portfolio diversifies when you pay your tax obligations. Taxes on a Roth IRA are paid as you contribute. All other retirement investments require taxes to be paid on withdrawals. Paying taxes up front could work out in your favor in the event that tax rates and brackets increase in the future. When you do begin to make withdrawals from your Roth IRA, you won't owe taxes on the amount taken out.

One of the big benefits of the Roth IRA is that your investment is allowed to grow tax-free. Investors in the higher tax brackets can use a Roth IRA to hold investments that produce a large proportion of short-term gains, dividends and interest. Outside the Roth IRA, these types of investments would be taxed as income, not at a favorable capital gains rate, when they are held less than 18 months. If you're in a high tax bracket, your income tax rate is higher than the capital gain tax rate. By putting these investments inside a Roth IRA where no taxes are paid on investment growth, you avoid paying the higher tax rate.

Dogs of the Dow is an investment strategy that turns over most of a portfolio's stocks on a yearly basis. Because gains are made in less than 12 months, this strategy triggers income taxes at the marginal tax rate rather than the potentially more favorable, long-term capital gains tax rates. Once again, if you are in a high tax bracket your income tax rate would be higher than the capital gains tax rate. You can see that this investment strategy would work well on investments held in a Roth IRA. Aggressive mutual fund portfolios that produce a significant amount of portfolio turnover and short-term capital gains, high dividend paying stocks such as utilities, preferred stocks, and corporate bonds also work well in a Roth IRA. Of course zero tax on any investment gain is better than any tax at all!

Roth vs. Non-Deductible IRA

Both a Roth IRA and a traditional, nondeductible IRA require taxes to be paid on contributions but allow the investment to grow tax deferred. The difference is that with a traditional, nondeductible IRA you pay taxes on the deferred portion of your investment when you make withdrawals during retirement. Qualified, tax deferred withdrawals from a Roth IRA are not taxed. The Roth IRA is obviously a much better choice than a traditional, nondeductible IRA for all who qualify.

Roth vs. Taxable, Non-IRA Investment

Now that capital gains rates have been lowered, you may wonder how well a taxable, non-IRA investment would compare to the Roth. Again the answer is a no-brainer. With a taxable account you pay taxes on contributions, investment growth and distributions. As you now know, with a Roth IRA you pay taxes on contributions but not on growth or withdrawals. The Roth IRA is obviously the better choice when it comes to investing for retirement.

Now since we covered the easy ones let's look at the other possibilities. The decision gets more difficult when comparing the Roth to the deductible contribution IRA.

Roth vs. Deductible IRA

The Roth IRA is obviously the better choice when compared to a nondeductible IRA or a taxable, non-IRA investment. The big question now is: Which is better, the Roth IRA or a traditional, deductible IRA? Intuitively, it may seem that the Roth is a better choice because you could have the two different types of IRA's with the same contribution level, the same growth and the same account value at retirement but the Roth distributions are tax-free. Without regard to any other factors, a $2,000 contribution to a Roth IRA is more valuable than a $2,000 contribution to a traditional IRA because there is no tax liability on the withdrawals. There are, however, other factors to consider.

When it comes to choosing between a Roth IRA and a traditional, deductible IRA, one is definitely a better choice than the other—which one depends on your individual situation. Many factors come into play including your current tax bracket, your tax bracket at retirement, your current investment position, how much cash you have available for investing, what your retirement income needs will be, how much you expect to get from other retirement investments, and how you intend to use the funds during retirement.

Let's start by reviewing how both the Roth IRA and the traditional, deductible IRA work. With a Roth IRA, your contributions are taxed but investment growth and qualified withdrawals are not. With a traditional, deductible IRA, your contributions are not taxed and taxes on investment contribution and growth is deferred until you make withdrawals. Taxes are paid up front with a Roth IRA. With a traditional, deductible IRA, taxes are paid at the end according to your marginal tax rate. So the question, once again, is whether it is better to pay taxes now or later. *To understand the rest of this discussion it is very important that you are familiar with the marginal tax rate system. Take this opportunity now, if you are not already comfortable with how the system works, to review Appendix A.*

Scenario #1 - Investor in the 28 percent tax bracket

Follow along in Tables 3.2 through 3.6 as we take a look at two investors, A and B. Both earn $60,000 per year and are in the 28 percent marginal tax bracket. Investor A makes a $2,000 pre-tax, deductible contribution to a traditional IRA while Investor B makes a $2,000 after-tax contribution to a Roth IRA. Table 3.2 shows that Investor A's $2,000 IRA contribution is subtracted from his gross income and Investor B's $2,000 Roth IRA contribution is subtracted after taxes are paid. Because of the deduction from gross, Investor A pays less in taxes and ends up with a $560 greater net income. Investor A is able to put $2,000 into an IRA and still end up with $560 more in his annual cash flow.

Investor A makes a $2,000 tax-deductible contribution to an IRA while investor B makes a $2,000 after-tax contribution to a Roth IRA. As you can see investor A has a $560 higher after-tax bottom line due to the pre-tax investment. This allows investor A to contribute $2,000 to a retirement investment, defer all taxes and have a $560 higher yearly cash flow than Investor B.

Table 3.2   Tax-Deductible Contributions Mean Greater Annual Cash Flow

	Investor A	Investor B	Difference
Gross Income	$60,000	$60,000	
IRA Deduction	$2,000	$0	
Other Deductions	$10,500	$10,500	
Total Deductions	$12,500	$10,500	
Taxable Income	$47,500	$49,500	
Tax Due at 15% Rate	$6,180	$6,180	
Tax Due at 28% Rate	$1,764	$2,324	($560)
Total Tax Due	$7,944	$8,504	($560)
After-Tax Income	$50,056	$51,496	($1440)
Roth Deduction	$0	$2,000	
After-Tax Bottom Line	$50,056	$49,496	$560

Investor A and Investor B both make a $2,000 contribution to an IRA. Investor A's contribution is tax-deferred, Investor B's is not. You can see that Investor A ends up with $560 more at the end of the year after paying taxes.

Investor A can make a $2,000 IRA contribution with $2,000 in earned income. Investor B needs $2,778 in earned income in order to make a $2,000 Roth IRA contribution because $778 goes toward taxes. Table 3.3 shows the $778 increase in gross income needed to give Investor B the same after-tax bottom line as investor A. Now, this is interesting. If Investor A's gross income is increased by $778 as well, he can invest that money into another tax-deferred investment, such as a 401(k), and still end up with the same after-tax bottom line as he did when his gross income and contribution were both $778 less. This means that with a gross income of $60,778, Investor A can get $778 more into his investment and still end up with

Table 3.3 Tax-Deductible vs. Non-Deductible Contributions

	Investor A	Investor B	Difference
Gross Income	$60,000	$60,778	(778)
IRA Deduction	$2,000	$0	
Deductions	$10,500	$10,500	
Total Deductions	$12,500	$10,500	
Taxable Income	$47,500	$50,278	
Tax Due at 15% Rate	$6,180	$6,180	
Tax Due at 28% Rate	$1,764	$2,541	($778)
Total Tax Due	$7,944	$8,722	($778)
After-Tax Income	$50,056	$52,056	($2,000)
Roth Deduction	$0	$2,000	
After-Tax Bottom Line	$50,056	$50,056	$0

Investor A and Investor B both make a $2,000 contribution to an IRA. Investor A's contribution is tax-deductible, Investor B's is not. It actually takes $2,778 for Investor B to contribute $2,000 to his IRA because his contribution is taxed. Investors A and B end up with the same bottom line but Investor A has $778 more that he can invest pre-tax elsewhere.

the same after-tax bottom line as Investor B who earned the same amount but was only able to contribute $2,000 to his Roth IRA.

The purpose of this last scenario is to show that you must take into account that Investor A is able to make a larger contribution each year and still end up with the same net, take-home earnings as Investor B. These larger, annual contributions need to be accounted for when comparing the overall outcome between the two types of IRA's.

Take a look at Table 3.4. It shows the growth of both investments where the contributions grow at 12 percent per year. Both investments have a $2,000 annual contribution growing at 12 percent, but Investor A also has an additional $778 growing at 12 percent. Of course the pre-tax IRA investment is going to be much larger because the contributions are larger. At the end of 40 years Investor A has $668,412 more than Investor B. Pretty amazing. Investor A had the same take-home pay as Investor B for 40 years, yet he ends up with $668,412 more money than Investor B by the time he retires! Notice that the spread in value between the two investments gets much larger as time goes by.

The story's not over yet. Investor A made more money—a lot more money, but now he owes taxes on the withdrawals and Investor B does not. So now which investment do you think comes out ahead? The mystery continues. Let's say that each IRA earns an annual 7 percent during retirement and that both investors plan to deplete their portfolio over a 25 year period. Assume also that all funds distributed from the pre-tax IRA are taxed at 28 percent. This will not always be the case because it depends on the investor's marginal tax rate.

Take a look at Table 3.5. When it comes time to take a withdrawal, Investor A can get $18,045 more because his account is so much bigger. But look out for those taxes! Once taxes are paid on Investor A's distribution, he ends up with just about the same amount of money as Investor B who had a smaller account but didn't have to pay taxes on the distributions. The reason that both investments ended up the same is because the tax rate used on the Roth IRA's *contributions* (28 percent) is the same as the tax rate used on the tax-deferred account's *distributions*.

Now, 28 percent was used in the above example just to show that the two taxing methods used end up producing the same account values. In the real world, distributions are taxed at the investor's *marginal* tax rate. Remember that this is not a flat tax rate. Let's say that Investor A's IRA distribution is his only taxable income. Table 3.6 shows that Investor A, taxed at marginal rates, ends up with $5,630 more each year. Look's

Table 3.4   Pre-Tax Savings Means More Money to Invest

Year	Roth IRA	Pre-Tax IRA	Pre-Tax Additional	Total Pre-Tax
1	$2,240	$2,240	$871	$3,111
2	$4,749	$4,749	$1,847	$6,596
3	$7,559	$7,559	$2,940	$10,499
4	$10,706	$10,706	$4,165	$14,870
5	$14,230	$14,230	$5,536	$19,766
10	$39,309	$39,309	$15,291	$54,600
15	$83,507	$83,507	$32,484	$115,991
20	$161,397	$161,397	$62,784	$224,181
25	$298,668	$298,668	$116,182	$414,850
30	$540,585	$540,585	$210,288	$750,873
35	$966,926	$966,926	$376,134	$1,343,061
40	$1,718,285	$1,718,285	$668,413	$2,386,698

This table shows the growth of a $2,000 annual contribution into a Roth IRA and into a traditional, tax-deductible IRA. Both investments grow at 12 percent. Remember that it takes $2,778 of earned income to make a $2,000 contribution into a Roth IRA if you are in the 28 percent tax bracket. It only takes $2,000 to make the same contribution into the pre-tax IRA which means that an extra $778 is available per year in tax savings. The third column in this table shows how this additional money will grow over time if it is invested at the same rate of 12 percent—it gives the investor an additional $668,412 at the end of 40 years!

Table 3.5 Final Comparison of Pre-Tax IRA and Roth IRA

	Pre - tax IRA	Roth IRA
Initial Portfolio Value	$750,837	$540,586
Distribution	$64,433	$46,388
Tax Due at 28%	$18,041	$0
After-Tax Distribution	$46,392	$46,388

This table compares the final outcome of a $2,000 per year contribution into both a traditional, tax-deductible IRA and a Roth IRA. Both investments are made over a 30 year period, grow at a rate of 12 percent, and are accumulated by an investor in the 28 percent tax bracket. At the end of 30 years the traditional IRA is valued at $750,837. The Roth IRA is worth $540,586. Although the traditional IRA grew to a larger account value, once taxes are paid on the distributions (the investor is still in the 28 percent tax bracket) the final value of the two IRA's ends up about the same. This is because the tax rate used on the Roth IRA's *contributions* is the same as the tax rate used on the tax-deferred account's *distributions*. The distribution is based on a 7 percent annual return and a 25 year period with zero value remaining.

like Investor A wins the competition after all! Please understand, however, that this is a very specific example. If Investor A had enough income from other sources, such as Social Security, pensions, 401(k), annuities, and other investments, he may end up in a higher tax bracket and end up owing more taxes on his distribution. In other words, the variables could change slightly to the point where Investor B comes out ahead.

The lesson learned from this scenario is that marginal tax brackets play a very big part in the final outcome of the two different types of IRA's. It is very important that you to take into account your current, future, and retirement tax brackets. In addition, tax brackets will likely be adjusted for inflation and perhaps even changed by congress.

Table 3.6 Final Comparison of Pre-Tax IRA and Roth IRA with Marginal Tax Bracket

	Pre - tax IRA	Roth IRA
Initial Portfolio Value	$750,837	$540,586
Distribution	$64,433	$46,388
Tax Due at Marginal Rates	$12,685	$0
After-Tax distribution	$51,748	$46,388

This table repeats the same scenario as shown in Table 3.5. The difference is that the distributions in Table 3.5 were taxed at a flat rate of 28 percent to show that both IRA's end up producing the same end result. In the real world, our tax system is marginal, not flat, which is what this table takes into account. 1998 tax rates are used. The first $41,200 is taxed at 15 percent. Using the marginal tax rate system, the traditional IRA comes out $5,630 ahead of the Roth IRA under the very specific conditions of this example.

Scenario #2 - Investor in the 15 percent tax bracket

Now let's take a look at Investors X and Y. Both are in the 15 percent tax bracket prior to retirement and both make annual contributions of $2,000. Investor X, however, contributes pre-tax to a traditional IRA and Investor Y makes taxable contributions to a Roth IRA. Since investor X is contributing pre-tax dollars he is able to defer $353 dollars more each year into another tax-favored account such as a 401(k) plan. He will still have the same after-tax bottom line as investor Y. So far, the scenario is the same as the one above except that Investor X only has an additional $353 dollars to work with rather than Investor A's $778. This is because we are now using the 15 percent tax bracket rather than the 28 percent tax bracket.

You learned earlier that if distributions from the traditional IRA are taxed at the same rate as contributions to the Roth IRA that the end result would be the same for both investments.

Table 3.7 Final Comparison of Pre-Tax IRA and Roth IRA Using 15 Percent Tax Rate

	Pre - tax IRA	Roth IRA
Initial Portfolio Value	$648,732	$540,586
Distribution	$55,668	$46,388
Tax Due at 15%	$8,350	$0
After-Tax Distribution	$47,317	$46,388

This table repeats the scenario shown in Table 3.5 with one change. The portfolio was accumulated by an investor in the 15 percent tax bracket then distributed at the 15 percent tax rate. Once again you can see that the final value of the accounts ends up being about the same.

You can see this principle at work once again in Table 3.7. Let's now make the scenario more interesting. Let's say that both investors end up in a higher tax bracket, 28 percent, when they retire. The Roth IRA will obviously be a better choice because no taxes are paid on distributions. The traditional IRA pays taxes at the 28 percent marginal tax rate on distributions whereas the Roth IRA only paid at the 15 percent marginal tax rate on contributions. Table 3.8 shows this affect.

The lesson here is that the Roth IRA is a better choice than the traditional, tax-deductible IRA if you expect to be in a higher tax bracket during retirement than you are in your working years. If you expect to drop to a lower tax bracket in your retirement years, than the traditional, tax-deductible IRA is the better choice. The Roth IRA and the traditional, tax-deductible IRA have opposite affects when it comes to applying tax rates to contributions and distributions.

Table 3.8   Final Comparison of Pre-Tax IRA and Roth IRA Using 15 and 28 Percent Tax Rates

	Pre - tax IRA	Roth IRA
Initial Portfolio Value	$648,732	$540,586
Distribution	$55,668	$46,388
Tax Due at 28%	$15,587	$0
After-Tax Distribution	$40,081	$46,388

This table repeats the scenario shown in Table 3.7 with one change. The portfolio was accumulated by an investor in the 15 percent tax bracket then distributed at the 28 percent tax rate. In this case, the Roth IRA is a better choice because no taxes are paid on distributions. The traditional IRA pays taxes at the 28 percent marginal rate on distributions whereas the Roth IRA only paid at the 15 percent marginal rate on contributions.

Benefits of Roth IRA

As mentioned earlier, the biggest appeal of the Roth IRA is that it can continue to grow throughout retirement. You are not required to take minimum withdrawals. Our example showed both IRA's distributed at retirement. Some individuals may not need or want to tap their IRA immediately during retirement. Or at all. In this case, the Roth IRA clearly shines as the better investment. The traditional IRA will typically force you to start minimum withdrawals at age 70 1/2. The distributions are considered ordinary income and taxed at the marginal tax rate. This may create a larger tax burden than pre 70 1/2 withdrawals. The Roth IRA will allow the continual tax free investment accumulation as long as the investor is alive. At death the Roth IRA must be distributed, but it is tax-free!

Another good feature of the Roth IRA is that you can pay taxes now and diversify your future tax liability. Pre-tax investments, such as the 401(k) and the traditional, tax-deductible IRA, only defer taxes. Instead of paying taxes up front, you pay them at the end—on withdrawals. Since there's no way to predict what the tax rates may be 20 to 30 years in the future, its a good idea to provide yourself with future income sources that are tax-free in order to offset income sources that are not tax-free. It works the other way as well. The tax climate may be such that tax-deferred investments end up providing a more favorable retirement income source than does the Roth IRA with it's tax-free withdrawals. Don't let this confuse you. Of course its always better to have an income source that's tax-free, all things being equal, but this is not the case. The tax-deferred investment gave you more money to work with in the early years because contributions were not taxed. This feature gives the tax-deferred investment the opportunity to grow at a faster rate, thereby, giving you a greater final account value. In any event, if the tax environment ends up such that its better to defer taxes until retirement, then you will be covered if you have a 401(k) or other pre-tax investment. If the tax environment ends up favoring investments that are taxed up front on contributions and not on withdrawals, then you will be covered if you have a Roth IRA. In other words, we don't know what will happen with taxes as the years go by so its better to prepare for both possible outcomes.

If you do decide to allow your Roth IRA to continue growing after you reach 70 1/2, then you are giving yourself a good inflation hedge. Yes, you still have to worry about inflation even after you retire because you could easily have another

---

Something to Consider

It is possible that the Roth IRA may be repealed or greatly limited at some time in the future. While nothing points to this happening any time soon, the IRA is the most trimmed and tucked piece of legislation I have ever seen. If this does happen, past contributions will probably be grandfathered in.

---

twenty or so years on your investment time horizon. Fixed income vehicles such as company pensions, annuities, and savings accounts lose purchasing power during retirement because of inflation. A Roth IRA invested in growth-orientated investments should easily be able to outpace inflation. Since the Roth IRA is allowed to grow tax-free, the accumulation will be substantial in the later years of your retirement. Additional income from your Roth IRA can be used to offset loss of income from other sources due to inflation.

Investments that Work Well In a Roth IRA

To make the most of any IRA, its a good idea to select investments with a high return such as growth stocks. Growth stocks perform well over the long term and the IRA is a long-term investment. With a Roth IRA, high dividend yielding investments are a good choice as well. Outside an IRA, these investments would be taxed at the marginal rate and would not be eligible for favorable capital gains rates. Inside the Roth, they grow tax-free and can later be withdrawn tax-free. You get the effective returns as shown in Table 3.9. When you make qualified withdrawals you have accumulated interest tax free that would have been taxable at a 28 percent or higher marginal tax rate. You have basically established a tax-free income fund that pays substantially higher rates. This is an excellent opportunity for higher income individuals to avoid taxes on the interest and dividends that would be taxed at the marginal rate during retirement.

Here is an example of a possible Roth IRA used to generate tax-free income. Table 3.10 shows the different after-tax values that could be achieved depending on the account value and tax rate. For investors in a higher tax bracket the Roth IRA can produce a high after tax return with moderate risk.

Table 3.9 Roth IRA Effective Returns

Rate of Return	28% Tax Bracket	31% Tax Bracket
6%	8.33%	8.69%
7%	9.72%	10.15%
8%	11.11%	11.59%
9%	12.50%	13.04%
10%	13.89%	14.49%

This table shows the effective rate of return you get by putting high dividend yielding investments in a Roth IRA in order to avoid marginal rate taxes. Column 1 shows the rate of return achieved outside the Roth where it is taxed. Column 2 shows the effective rate of return achieved by an investor in the 28 percent tax bracket when the same investment is placed in a Roth. Column 3 is the same as Column 2 except it is for an investor in the 31 percent tax bracket.

Table 3.10 Dollar Value of Effective Returns

Account Value	28% Tax Bracket	31% Tax Bracket	Tax-Free
$50,000	$2,880	$2,760	$4,000
$75,000	$4,320	$4,140	$6,000
$100,000	$5,760	$5,520	$8,000

This table shows what you would earn from an investment with the dollar value shown in column 1 if it is taxed at the 28 percent, 31 percent and 0 percent rate. The 0 percent rate is available if the investment is placed in a Roth IRA. Rate of return is 8 percent.

Chapter 4

The Educational IRA

The Educational IRA is somewhat misleading in terms of how we think an IRA works. It is actually used to invest tax-free for a child's college educational expenses. It is not a retirement investment and your contributions are not tax-deductible. All funds must be disbursed by the time the beneficiary turns 30. As you know, both the traditional IRA and the Roth IRA are not generally disbursed until retirement age. The Educational IRA is similar to the Roth IRA in that contributions are taxable, contribution limitations are placed on certain income levels, investment growth is not taxed, and withdrawals are tax-free if certain conditions are followed.

The Educational IRA may be established for any child under 18 years of age. It is set up as a trust arrangement with the child as beneficiary. Contributions are taxable and limited to $500 per year per child. Anyone can contribute to the account as long as total annual contributions are limited to $500 per child. The accumulated tax-deferred earnings may be withdrawn tax-free to pay for post secondary educational expenses.

Overall, the Educational IRA is a very good way to save for a child's educational expenses because it allows your earnings to grow tax-free. Of course, as with all good opportunities, certain restrictions apply.

Basic Features of the Educational IRA

- Provides a tax-favored way to invest for a child's college educational expenses.

- A maximum of $500 can be contributed per year.

- Contributions can be made until the child reaches age 18.

- Contributions are not tax-deductible.

- Contributions may be made by anyone (aunts, uncles, grandparents, parents, etc.).

- Limitations are placed on contributions from married taxpayers who earn above $150,000 and from single tax-payers who earn above $95,000.

- Distributions are not taxed if the money is used for educational expenses.

- Distributions must be made by the time the child reaches age 30.

- Distributions not used for educational expenses are taxed as ordinary income *and* are subject to a 10 percent penalty.

- You may not take Educational IRA distributions in the same year a Hope Scholarship Credit or a Lifetime Learning Credit is used.

- An Educational IRA may be rolled over to another Educational IRA belonging to another family member.

- The beneficiary of an Educational IRA can be changed to another family member.

Trust Agreement

The Educational IRA is a trust arrangement created for a child who is named beneficiary. It must be established for the sole purpose of paying qualified educational expenses for the beneficiary. Any qualified trust agent, such as a bank, mutual fund, broker, or other agency, may set up an Educational IRA for you. Make sure the trustee understands that the IRA is to be structured as an Educational IRA. The Educational IRA will probably not be offered by all eligible institutions.

Are You Eligible?

Anyone may contribute money to an Educational IRA up to the limit of $500 per year per child if their Adjusted Gross Income (AGI) is under $95,000 for single filers and under $150,000 for married filers. Contribution levels are phased out as income rises above these limits. All contributions must be made in cash. See Table 4.1 for an overview of phaseout limits.

As mentioned earlier, contributions may come from a parent, uncle, aunt, or friend as long as total contributions do not exceed $500 per year. Contribution levels are not affected by whether or not the beneficiary has earned income. Money

Table 4.1 Contribution Limits for the Educational IRA

Single Filer	Contribution	Married Filer	Contribution
$95,000	$500	$150,000	$500
$98,000	$400	$152,000	$400
$101,000	$300	$154,000	$300
$104,000	$200	$156,000	$200
$107,000	$100	$158,000	$100
$110,000	$0	$160,000	$0

This table shows an overview of how much you can contribute to an Educational IRA based on your income level and your tax filing status. For example, if you are a single filer you are only eligible for the full $500 annual contribution if your income level is $95,000 or below.

may be added to the account until the child reaches 18 years of age. Contributions are *not* tax-deductible.

If you've read the previous chapters on the traditional and Roth IRA's, you may remember that you can only contribute a total of $2,000 into all of your IRA's per year. This limitation does not include the Educational IRA. For example, you can contribute $1,000 to a traditional IRA, $1,000 to a Roth IRA, plus an additional $500 per child to an Educational IRA all in the same year. In other words, if you use an Educational IRA and you have two children you can actually contribute $3,000 per year into IRA accounts. Out of that $3,000, $2,000 goes into your own IRA account and $500 goes into each of the children's Educational IRA for a total of $1,000.

Here's another example. Aunt Mandy, who is single, has an Adjusted Gross Income of less than $95,000. She contributes $500 into her niece Maggie's Educational IRA. The contribution is not tax-deductible. She may still contribute $2,000 into her own IRA within her personal IRA qualifications. The $500 has no affect on her own IRA eligibility. Also, since Aunt Mandy contributed $500 into little Maggie's IRA, no one else may make contributions on behalf of Maggie for that year.

You may have more than one IRA set up as an Educational IRA for the same beneficiary but the total of all contributions may not exceed $500 in any one year. This may come in handy if Uncle George wants his contributions to be invested in a different IRA than the one Aunt Mandy used the year earlier. Here's another caution. No contribution can be made to an Educational IRA in the same year that money is contributed to a qualified state tuition program for the same beneficiary.

Distributions

Distributions from an Educational IRA are not taxed if they are used to pay for qualified educational expenses. Qualified expenses include books, tuition, fees, supplies, and equipment. Room and board is an allowed expense if the beneficiary is enrolled at least half time or is taking at least half the normal course load of a full-time student.

The educational institution attended by the beneficiary must meet certain eligibility requirements. These requirements are the same as those needed to participate in any of the student aid programs administered by the Department of Education. Almost every accredited public, nonprofit, or private post secondary institution is included.

Caution: The room and board expenses have a restriction that the beneficiary must be enrolled in an eligible institution and carry at least one-half the normal course load for the degree being pursued. The room and board expenses for students living off campus are limited. Other qualified expenses do not have the course load restriction.

Qualified expenses that can be paid by the Educational IRA are reduced by the amount of funds received from a scholarship or grant. You cannot use Educational IRA distributions in the same year that a Hope Scholarship Credit or a Lifetime Learning Credit is used. Let's look at an example. Mary has accumulated $3,000 worth of educational expenses. In the same year, she received a $500 scholarship. The expenses eligible for a qualified distribution from her Educational IRA is $2,500 because the original $3,000 expense was reduced by the $500 scholarship. A Hope or Lifetime learning credit cannot be claimed.

Remember that all of the money in an Educational IRA must be used before the beneficiary reaches age 30. If the funds are not used for educational expenses by this time, then they must be distributed to the beneficiary as ordinary income. Not only do you pay ordinary income taxes on this type of withdrawal, there is also a 10 percent penalty. You can avoid the penalty and the tax by rolling the IRA into an Educational IRA belonging to another qualified family member.

The trust agreement requires that if the beneficiary dies, any balance in the account must be distributed to the beneficiary's estate within 30 days after death.

Rollovers

As you just learned, an Educational IRA may be rolled over in part or all into an Educational IRA belonging to a qualified family member. You may also change who the beneficiary of an Educational IRA is as long as the new person is a qualified family member. In addition, if you want the money in your Educational IRA to be invested elsewhere you can roll it over into another Educational IRA with a new trustee. The rollover must be made within 60 days.

Rollovers are not limited to the $500 per year contribution limit. Any amount may be rolled over from one Educational IRA to another Educational IRA as long as the new IRA belongs to the same beneficiary or to a qualified family member.

Let's say that Mr. And Mrs. Smart have established Educational IRA's for their two children, Penny and Spencer. After several years of contributing have gone by and the IRA has grown in value, Penny turns 18. She is now no longer eligible to receive contributions. Meanwhile, Spencer is only 14 so his IRA continues to receive contributions. Penny has $2,000 worth of educational expenses in her first year of college. She had already withdrawn $2,200 from her Educational IRA in order to cover anticipated expenses. Since she withdrew $200 more than was needed, a portion of the excess is subject to ordinary income taxes and to a 10 percent penalty. If the withdrawal had been made less than 60 days ago, Penny may roll the excess $200 into Spencer's Educational IRA or she may put it back into her own Educational IRA in order to avoid the tax and penalty.

Now let's say that after one year of college Penny receives a full scholarship that covers all qualified educational expenses. Since she will no longer have any qualified educational expenses she may roll her IRA into Spencer's. Since the money is a rollover between Educational IRA's it is not limited to the $500 contribution amount. Spencer may continue to receive contributions up to the annual $500 limit until he turns

18. He may also continue to receive qualified Educational IRA rollovers from other family members at any time. Because Penny received a full scholarship, Mr. and Mrs. Smart are able to get much more money into Spencer's account by rolling the balance of Penny's account into his.

Things to Consider

Keep in mind that an Educational IRA contribution is limited to $500 per year per child. Because contributions can be made until the beneficiary turns 18, the maximum amount that can be added to a child's account is $9,000. This can be accomplished by contributing $500 per year to the child's account starting at birth and continuing for 18 years. You can see that it will take several years to accumulate a significant amount of money. Starting an Educational IRA for a child near 18 years of age does not give you a good investment opportunity. Tax-deferred investing works best when you have a long time horizon to work with because you need time for investment gains to accumulate. What makes the Educational IRA attractive is the tax-free accumulation of investment gains. Contributions are not tax-deductible. Table 4.2 compares what the final value of your account will be worth if you contribute $500 a year for 1 to 18 years. For the illustration, an annual rate of return of 12 percent is used.   As you can see, tax free compounding does not produce significant gains for at least 5 to 10 years. An Educational IRA started for a 14 year old will not produce significant gains by the time the child turns 18. Even if you wait until the child turns 22 to use the funds, the accumulation will not be significant because contributions must stop at age 18.

The Educational IRA is best suited for young children. By starting early, you give yourself plenty of time for growth and you free up more years to contribute. It is also important to go after high rates of return in order to further magnify the tax-free accumulation of investment gains. Table 4.3 compares what the final value of your account will be using 8 percent and

Table 4.2 Early vs. Late Contributions

Year	Early	Middle	Late
1	$560		
2	$1,187		
3	$1,890		
4	$2,676		
5	$3,558		
6	$4,545		
7	$5,650		
8	$6,888	$560	
9	$8,274	$1,187	
10	$9,827	$1,890	
11	$11,567	$2,676	
12	$13,515	$3,558	
13	$15,696	$4,545	
14	$18,140	$5,650	$560
15	$20,877	$6,888	$1,187
16	$23,942	$8,274	$1,890
17	$27,375	$9,827	$2,676
18	$31,220	$11,567	$3,558

This table shows what the final value of your account will be if you contribute $500 a year to an Educational IRA. The column labeled "Early" shows what happens when you start the IRA when your child is born. The column labeled "Middle" starts when your child is 8 years old. The column labeled "Late" starts when your child is 14 years old. All three illustrations assume contributions are made at the beginning of the year and grow at the rate of 12 percent.

12 percent rates of return. Of course the higher rate of return produces better investment results. For this reason, it makes sense to invest in equities.

If your children are 14 years or older, the Educational IRA may not be an effective investment tool. Other options, such as the Hope Credit, Lifelong Learning Credit, and prepaid tuition may prove to be better opportunities for your situation. In this case, you could put your money into your own IRA and pay for future tuition out-of-pocket. The Hope Scholarship Credit and the Lifelong Learning Credit both give you a tax credit. You can also withdraw money penalty-free from your own IRA if needed. This option is not recommended but its nice to know that the money is available if needed and if your child decides not to go to college then your IRA keeps growing. Remember, withdrawals from the traditional IRA will be taxed as ordinary income. Withdrawals from the Roth IRA are tax-free but cannot be made until the IRA is five years old.

Tip: Coordinate the use of the Hope Scholarship Credit and Educational IRA. The Hope Scholarship Credit allows for a $1,500 tax credit for at least $2,000 of expenses for a student. It is limited to the first two years of post secondary education and can not be used with the Educational IRA. Consider using the Hope Scholarship for the first two years while the Educational IRA grows. Then use the Educational IRA for the remaining years. This works very well if the student first goes to a local junior college where expenses may be smaller then onto a major college.

There are a few challenges when looking for an investment to set up the Educational IRA. Since the amount of money you can contribute is small many investment funds will not pursue your investment. The most you can invest is $500 per year per child. This is not a very big enticement for investment funds, especially the low-load, low-expense type funds. The ones that will offer it may charge larger fees and have specific restrictions. There may be a fixed account fee for the Educational IRA. This may be in addition to or due to setting up the Educational IRA. The funds may require a minimum investment

Table 4.3 $500 Annual Contributions Growing at 8 percent and 12 percent

Year	Contribution	8% Growth	12% Growth
1	$500	$540	$560
2	$500	$1,123	$1,187
3	$500	$1,753	$1,890
4	$500	$2,433	$2,676
5	$500	$3,168	$3,558
6	$500	$3,961	$4,545
7	$500	$4,818	$5,650
8	$500	$5,744	$6,888
9	$500	$6,743	$8,274
10	$500	$7,823	$9,827
11	$500	$8,989	$11,567
12	$500	$10,248	$13,515
13	$500	$11,607	$15,696
14	$500	$13,076	$18,140
15	$500	$14,662	$20,877
16	$500	$16,375	$23,942
17	$500	$18,225	$27,375
18	$500	$20,223	$31,220

This table shows what the final value of your Educational IRA will be at the end of 18 years if you contribute $500 a year and the investment is allowed to grow at 8 percent and 12 percent.

amount. It will probably be the $500 maximum allowed contribution. They should not ask for more because it is not allowed. They may also require it to be paid as a single payment and not spread out over a few months or as an automatic deposit. You may be offered only a few funds to choose from. They may be the less than desirable performing funds which need assets. A poor fund will cancel the benefits of a good investment vehicle very fast.

Since the Educational IRA is a trust and your account balance will be small you should expect to pay a minimum $10 per year trust fee with no-load funds and up to $100 dollars account fee with full commission brokers. Many no-loads waive the trust fee when the account reaches a certain minimum balance. This is usually around $5,000. You will not have this much money for probably at least five years. Be careful of all fees when setting up an Educational IRA. Pay special attention to the fixed account fee. This is a fixed fee levied against your account regardless of asset value and fund performance. Table 4.4 shows how the fixed account fee affects your earnings potential. As you can see, a fee of $35 per year has a large affect on the investment growth of an Educational IRA. You can lose about $2,000 in gains by having a fixed fee over the life of the investment. This is like losing four years worth of contributions. If the fee is higher or gains lower you will lose even more to the fixed fee. Be very careful to check all expenses with special attention to any fixed account fee. You want to achieve high investment returns with low expenses in order to be successful with an Educational IRA.

Table 4.4 Effect of Fixed Account Fees on Growth of Educational IRA

Year	12% growth	12% growth with $35 account fee	Difference
1	$560	$525	$35
2	$1,187	$1,113	$74
3	$1,890	$1,772	$118
4	$2,676	$2,509	$167
5	$3,558	$3,335	$222
6	$4,545	$4,260	$284
7	$5,650	$5,297	$353
8	$6,888	$6,457	$430
9	$8,274	$7,757	$517
10	$9,827	$9,213	$614
11	$11,567	$10,844	$723
12	$13,515	$12,670	$845
13	$15,696	$14,715	$981
14	$18,140	$17,006	$1,134
15	$20,877	$19,572	$1,305
16	$23,942	$22,445	$1,496
17	$27,375	$25,664	$1,711
18	$31,220	$29,269	$1,951

This table shows how much value your Educational IRA loses each year as the result of a $35 annual account fee.

Investment Tips for the Educational IRA

- Best if started early. Only $500 per year allowed.

- Try to make contributions at the beginning of the year to increase your growth period.

- Look for good growth funds.

- Watch out for fixed account fees. Expect to pay a $10 trust fee.

- Not many funds will want to bother with the Educational IRA because contributions are so small.

- Funds may restrict you to only one single contribution of $500 each year.

How to Start an Educational IRA

To start an educational IRA, call the fund families you are interested in investing with. Request an application for the Educational IRA and prospectuses on funds you are interested in. If you are opening accounts for several children you will need to fill out a separate trust agreement per child. Read the application and agreement carefully. Select the best fund to fit your strategy. Fill out the trust agreement and return with check and fund selection. In a few days you will get confirmation of your investment.

T-Rowe Price and Janus no-load funds will allow you to set up an IRA directly with them. Charles Schawb and Waterhouse offer Educational IRA's which may be invested through their no-load mutual fund networks. You may be restricted as to which funds in the network you can invest in because the investment contribution of an Educational IRA is small. The $500 contribution will not satisfy all mutual fund minimum investment requirements. You can also purchase individual stocks for your Educational IRA through a discount broker.

Strategies and Implementation

The Educational IRA works very well for children who are very young. The limited contribution amount requires a substantial time period of growth and contributions to be effective for financing educational expenses. If you are struggling to fund your own retirement consider the following IRA strategy.

Bill and Jan have three children. They are considering opening an educational IRA for them. Bill and Jan both have IRA's but only contribute $500 per year. Instead of contributing into the educational IRA, Bill and Jan should consider increasing their IRA contributions by $1,500 with their funds. Let the grandparents and Aunts and Uncles contribute to the children's educational IRA. When the children are old enough for college, funds may be removed from the parent's IRA if required. If not, the retirement IRA funds will continue to grow.

Many times other financing becomes available for children's education. This may include scholarships, grants, or out-of-pocket payments if the parent's cash flow increases. If the child decides not to go to college then you have the concern of how to transfer or distribute the funds to a different beneficiary. If you are struggling to fund your retirement, losing control of money in educational IRA's may not be the best move for you.

As mentioned earlier, you may find it difficult to set up an Educational IRA because there's not much money involved in it. Several mutual fund companies plan to add this service in the future but it hasn't happened yet. Other companies may not get involved at all. At this printing, T-Rowe Price and Janus Funds have put in place the service to allow investors to set up an educational IRA. They have many good funds to chose from.

Discount brokers, Waterhouse and Charles Schwab, offer educational IRA's. Mutual funds that do not provide the educational IRA service directly may be accessed from the discount broker. You still need to find a fund that allows the

$500 minimum IRA initial investment. There are a few funds, such as Tweedy Brown Value and the Kaufman fund, that meet this requirement. Schwab does not have Tweedy Brown in their transaction-free network but Waterhouse does.

As you can see, it will require some work to get the Educational IRA established for your children. You will find that taking advantage of the opportunity is time well spent. A good place to start is with the **Kaufman Fund** (800-237-0132) and **Waterhouse** (800-934-4410) for an aggressive approach and **Tweedy Brown Value** (via Waterhouse) and **T-Rowe Price Equity Income** (800-638-5660) for a solid growth approach. Ask for an Educational IRA application and prospectus for the mutual funds you are interested in. Be sure to ask about fees or anything else you would like to know. The services reps are there to assist you.

All About the New IRA

Chapter 5

Create an IRA Strategy that Works

401(k) vs. IRA

How does an IRA compare to a 401(k) plan? This is a question that sooner or later must get tackled. I am very much in favor of the 401(k). It provides many opportunities to build wealth for retirement (see my book entitled *How to Build Wealth with your 401(k)*). In most cases, the IRA should be used as a complement to your 401(k). Because contributions are limited to $2,000 per year, the IRA may not give you enough savings for retirement on its own. Its best to use an IRA in addition to your 401(k) plan. There are situations, however, when a 401(k) plan has not been set up to properly provide a good investment opportunity. One of the ways this can happen is if your plan is set up as a variable annuity or the investment choices are lousy (refer to my book entitled *How to Build Wealth with your 401(k)*). In this case, a tax-deductible, traditional IRA can be used as a substitute, rather than a complement, for your 401(k).

When it comes to 401(k) investing, the most important strategy is to contribute enough money to get matching funds from your employer—if this benefit is available. In most, but not all cases, matching funds will overcome any inherent deficiencies in the way your plan is structured. If your plan is structured properly, matching funds provide an incredible boost to the final value of your account. Think of it as free money or as a raise that you don't have to ask for.

You can choose either a Roth IRA or a tax-deductible, traditional IRA as a complement to your plan. Be sure to include investments in your IRA that are not available within your 401(k) plan. If you are in one of the higher tax brackets and are not eligible for a deductible IRA, go for the Roth. If you are in a high tax bracket and have only $2,000 to contribute, consider the pre-tax 401(k). In most cases, you should contribute the maximum amount allowed in your 401(k) before pursuing an IRA.

Strategy is Important

For those that know me, I always stress that building a strategy is the most important part of investing. It is the road map for investment success. An IRA can be used to satisfy different needs as specified by different strategies. For some it may be an investment foundation, for others it is icing on the cake. No matter what your situation, properly integrating the best IRA choice into you overall investment strategy is important.

We have already reviewed in detail the types of available IRA's and how each option works. By now you can clearly see that each type of IRA has unique features and that a one-size-fits-all option is not available. The key is to examine your present situation with respect to IRA eligibility, marginal tax rates, retirement income needs, 401(k)'s, pensions, investment time horizon, current savings rate, and available cash flow for investing. From here you can select the IRA that will bring the greatest success to your portfolio.

Traditional, Non-Deductible IRA has Lost its Appeal

The traditional, nondeductible IRA has lost its appeal for almost all investors. If you want to contribute to a nondeductible IRA, the Roth IRA is a better choice as long as you qualify. The only time it makes sense to use a nondeductible, traditional IRA is if your salary level prevents you from qualifying for a Roth IRA or for a tax-deductible, traditional IRA. If you fit this situation you are probably in the 31 percent tax bracket. Even if the nondeductible IRA is your only choice, you won't get much help because contributions are not tax-deferred and distributions will be taxed at the marginal rate.

There's no need to spend any more time evaluating the traditional, nondeductible IRA. There just aren't any advantages to it in light of the new Roth IRA. From here on out, let's concentrate on the traditional, tax-deductible IRA and the new Roth IRA. To make the best decision, you will need to carefully examine the following areas: your marginal tax brackets now, in the future, and when you retire; other tax-deferred investments, your income needs during retirement, how many years until you retire, and your after-tax cash flow. Let's get started.

Tax Brackets

What do you suppose determines the amount of money you save when you defer taxes? The answer is easy. Its your marginal tax rate. This is also the rate that determines the amount of taxes you pay on taxable withdrawals from an IRA. As you can guess, an investor in the 28 percent marginal tax bracket benefits more from a pre-tax investment than does a 15 percent investor. On the other hand, someone in the 15 percent tax bracket pays less taxes on IRA withdrawals than does the investor in the 28 percent tax bracket.

Keep in mind that you may either jump to a higher tax bracket or fall to a lower one if your salary level changes substantially in either direction as time goes by. Any change in your tax bracket can be used to determine which IRA best fits your needs. If you expect to be in a higher tax bracket in the future it makes sense to pay off your tax commitment early when your tax rate is lower. This can be accomplished with a Roth IRA because taxes are paid on contributions, not on withdrawals. If, on the other hand, you expect to drop to a lower tax rate in the future the best option is to defer taxes until that time. In this case, the traditional, tax-deductible IRA is the best choice because taxes on contributions are deferred until you make withdrawals. Its also a good idea to bulk up on as many pre-tax investments (such as 401(k) plans) as possible if you are in one of the higher tax brackets. As an added note, if your tax bracket remains the same and you pay the same amount of taxes on contributions as you do on withdrawals, than the Roth IRA and the traditional, deductible IRA will produce the same results.

As you know, the tax bracket you are in during retirement plays an important role today in selecting which IRA best fits your needs. Unfortunately, it is very difficult to determine what this tax bracket will be. First of all, there's no telling what the marginal tax bracket ranges will be in the future. For example, in 1998 a married filer pays 15 percent on the first $41,200 of taxable income but in a few years this may be increased to 15 percent on the first $46,000 to adjust for inflation. We really don't even know if the ranges will be increased as time goes by. They may actually be lowered. Currently the tax rates are 15 percent, 28 percent, and 31 percent but this is not set in stone. The longer the time horizon the more difficult it is to predict what will happen.

How Will You Use Your IRA Funds?

Take time now, if you haven't already done so, to think about how you will use your IRA funds during retirement. If you have income coming from other sources, such as a pension or 401(k) plan, then you may not need money from your IRA right away. If this describes your situation, then the Roth IRA has one very big benefit—you can keep your money fully invested for as long as you want. With the traditional IRA you are required to begin taking minimum withdrawals at age 70 1/2. Can you see why its such a big advantage to let your Roth continue to grow? The longer it grows, the bigger it will get. The big advantage, however, is that you get to decide when additional money from an IRA is needed to make up for depleted funds from other investments. An added benefit is that withdrawals from a Roth IRA are not taxed. This allows you to avoid tax burdens in your later years.

You probably remember from previous discussions that a Roth IRA and a traditional, tax-deductible IRA will produce the same results if your tax bracket is the same during retirement as it is during your working years when you make contributions. If this situation applies to you, then it is even more important to determine whether or not you can take advantage of the Roth IRA feature that allows you to continue investing without withdrawals for as long as you want.

For investors who have access to and continue to build a substantial 401(k) or other pre-tax retirement plans, the Roth IRA is very attractive. This is especially the case if your salary is too high to qualify for the pre-tax IRA.

How Far Are You From Retirement?

Time is crucial in all respects of investing because of its effect on compound interest. If you are far from retirement, it is difficult to predict variables such as future tax rates and future retirement needs.

After-Tax Cash Flow

The amount of money you have available to invest for retirement is another factor that can help you decide which IRA to use. If you are in the 28 percent bracket and can barely pull together a few thousand dollars to invest per year, then the traditional, tax-deductible IRA is the better option. This is because pre-tax contributions allow you to get more money into your investment per each contribution. If cash flow is not a problem for you and funds are readily available to invest then the Roth IRA has an edge.

This is probably a good time to remind you that conversion from a pre-tax IRA to a Roth IRA requires payment of taxes on the taxable money converted into the Roth. A $100,000 conversion will require $28,000 in tax payments if you are in the 28 percent tax bracket. This is a heck of a lot of money to come up with so be sure to account for it.

Other Tax-Deferred Investments

Be sure to take into account all the other tax-deferred investments available to you as you make your IRA selection. You need to have an idea of how much income all your investments will provide when it comes time for you to retire. You also need to be aware of your future tax liabilities. You may not already know this but a traditional company pension is taxable at retirement. So are all the other tax-deferred investments such as a 401(k) plan, profit sharing plan, traditional IRA, and ESOP. A profit sharing plan is a wonderful benefit if your company offers it. It tends to sit quietly off to the side and can build up to a substantial final value over your working years.

If you have a significant amount of tax-deferred investments waiting for you at retirement, you may find the Roth IRA favorable. Since qualified withdrawals from a Roth IRA are not taxable, they will help take the edge off of taxes owed on other income sources. It will not be uncommon for more and more investors to have very large 401(k)'s at retirement. This is a wonderful opportunity but it also means that many of these investors will find themselves in the 28 percent tax bracket during retirement. Tax-free withdrawals from a Roth IRA will certainly be appreciated if you get bumped into a higher tax bracket at retirement.

Many of today's retirees are living comfortably on company pensions, Social Security and personal savings without having to tap into their IRA. When they reach age 70 1/2 they will be required to take minimum distributions from their IRA whether they want to or not. This is where a Roth IRA comes in handy. If you don't need the income right away, you can let it continue to grow tax-free. This helps offset the affects of inflation on your other investments and gives you a safety net of additional income in the later years of retirement.

Investors today who are far from retirement will probably have a different mix of investments to rely on when they retire. They will likely have large 401(k) plans, profit sharing plans and ESOP's rather than a company pension plan and Social Security. Today's investors will probably roll their retirement accounts into a traditional IRA at, or prior to, retirement. The combination of these newer investments can easily exceed the value of accounts held by older retirees. The IRA will likely be the major source of retirement income in the future. For some investors, the IRA may even produce enough income to put them in a much higher tax bracket at retirement (this is not a bad thing). Once again, a Roth IRA can be a complementary investment to help offset tax liabilities in this situation.

If you don't have access to tax-deferred investments such as a 401(k) plan or an ESOP then the traditional, tax-deferred IRA may be more helpful than the Roth IRA. The pre-tax IRA allows you to get more money into your investment because contributions are not taxed. If you do, however, have access to a 401(k) plan, you can contribute more on a yearly basis to this investment than to an IRA which restricts you to $2,000 per year.

As you can see, many factors come into play as you evaluate which IRA will best fit your situation. Table 5.1 has an overview of the main criteria involved. I think you will find it very helpful in making your decision. The suggestions, however, are not cut in stone. Your final decision should be based on all the information you have gathered that fits your specific situation.

There are many ways to invest using an IRA. You're contribution is limited to an aggregate of $2,000 per year across all IRA's. The exception is the Educational IRA which allows you to contribute an extra $500 per year per child. The Education IRA contribution does not affect your $2,000 IRA contribution eligibility. Depending on your tax bracket and investment strategy, the IRA has something to offer almost all investors. Choose your investment wisely and be sure to take advantage of the new IRA features as best as you can!

Let's take a look at a few sample scenarios.

Real-life Ways to Use an IRA

Stephen and Sophia are married and have a MAGI under $150,000. Their combined income is $100,000 and they both have 401(k)'s at work. They contribute the maximum amount to their 401(k)'s and have built up a substantial, pre-tax investment portfolio. Since Stephen and Sophia have a high level of after-tax cash flow, they are looking for opportunities to invest more of this money for retirement. They do not qualify for the tax-deductible IRA because of their income level so they are considering a nondeductible IRA or even a variable annuity.

The Roth IRA is an easy choice for this situation. Stephen and Sophia have already taken full advantage of their 401(k)'s and still have funds available to invest for retirement. In addition, they will probably be in the same tax bracket once they retire. The Roth IRA is a good complement to their 401(k) investments. They can now invest $4,000 ($2,000 each) into Roth IRA's which will be disbursed tax-free at retirement without concern for mandatory withdrawals.

Table 5.1 IRA Comparison

	Current Tax Bracket		Retirement Tax		Tax-Deferred Investment Options		Use of Funds		After-Tax Cash Vehicles		
	28%	15%	28%	15%	401(k), pension	none (or small)	early	late (after 70 1/2)	High	Moderate	
Roth IRA		X	X		X		X	X	X	X	STRONG ROTH
		X	X			X	X	X	X	X	STRONG ROTH
		X		X	X			X	X	X	
X			X			X			X	X		
X			X				X		X	X		
		X		X		X	X	X	X	X	MILD ROTH
Tax-Deductible IRA	X		X			X	X			X	MILD DEDUCTIBLE
X			X		X		X			X	X	
X				X	X		X		X			
X				X		X	X		X	X		
X				X		X	X		X	X	STRONG DEDUCTIBLE
X				X	X			X	X	X	STRONG DEDUCTIBLE

This table gives a quick look at the IRA that best fits your situation. Find the row that has x's in the column corresponding to your current tax bracket, the tax bracket you expect to be in when you retire, your tax deferred investment position, when you expect to use your IRA funds, and whether your holdings in after-tax cash investments is high or moderate.

Matt and Margo are married and have a MAGI under $150,000. Their combined income is $100,000. Both have 401(k)'s at work but they are not contributing the maximum allowed. They wish to build up a nice-sized nest egg for retirement. Their after-tax cash flow is moderate and they are in the 28 percent tax bracket. They do not qualify for the tax-deductible IRA. Matt and Margo are considering either a nondeductible IRA or even a variable annuity.

The recommendation here is that Matt and Margo take full advantage of their 401(k) before investing in something else. Contributions to a 401(k) are pre-tax so they can get an extra 28 percent into their accounts each year. If they still have after-tax funds available for investing, then the Roth IRA is the best choice.

Sonya has recently graduated from college and has started a job that will give her significant income growth in the years ahead. She is single and earns $40,000 per year. Expenses associated with college and with starting a new job have piled up. As a result, her after-tax cash flow is small. In addition, her job offers no retirement plan. Fortunately, Sonya is eligible for a traditional, tax-deductible IRA since she does not have a company retirement plan.

The pre-tax IRA is better for Sonya than the Roth IRA. She can contribute $2,000 pre-tax and still have a better after-tax return then if she used the Roth IRA. This tax savings can be used to build a money market fund for short-term needs outside of a retirement vehicle. Once her cash flow increases, she can reevaluate her long-term needs. If Sonya does not have a company retirement plan by this time, then the pre-tax IRA may still be the best opportunity for her.

Karen is 23 and earns $25,000 per year. Her income is expected to grow substantially over time. She has both a 401(k) plan with matching contributions and a company pension plan. Karen is eligible for a pre-tax IRA because of her income level. Her pre-tax savings would be 15 percent. In other words, since Karen is in the 15 percent tax bracket she defers, or saves, 15 percent in taxes on her contributions. This is a savings of $150 per $1,000.

In Karen's case, the Roth IRA may be a good strategic move. She is contributing pre-tax to her 401(k) and has a company pension plan that is also pre-tax. Pension plans are tax deductible to the company. The tax liability is on the recipient at retirement. Contributions to the Roth IRA are not pre-tax but she has already taken full advantage of other pre-tax investments. The Roth IRA gives her the added ability to let funds grow past age 70 1/2. This will work in her favor because the 401(k) and pension plan will probably provide for her initial retirement needs. In addition, Karen will probably be in either the same or a higher tax bracket during retirement. All-in-all, the Roth IRA fits well into Karen's situation.

Veronica is 28 and earns $24,000 per year. She has a 401(k) at work that matches contributions up to $1,000. Veronica has a good after-tax cash flow and expects her salary to increase over the years so that she will eventually be in the 28 percent tax bracket. Veronica contributes $1,000 to her 401(k) in order to get the matching funds. She also contributes a full $2,000 to a Roth IRA. This is a good move because it allows her to build a tax-free retirement account for the future when she will be in the 28 percent tax bracket. In addition, the after-tax portion of her contributions are taxed at the 15 percent marginal rate. Since Roth IRA contributions are after-tax, she has to earn an extra $353 in earned income to make the $2,000 contribution. When she is in the 28 percent tax bracket, a Roth IRA contribution of $2,000 will require $778 of additional earned income. Once her income increases to the 28 percent marginal rate, she can shift contributions away from the Roth IRA and into her 401(k) which will defer taxes at 28 percent. The Roth IRA will continue to grow tax-free and avoid the 28 percent tax rate on gains. This strategic move works very well for young investors.

Melissa and Ben are in their late fifties. They are in the 28 percent tax bracket and have company retirement plans and a 401(k). They would like to contribute to a Roth IRA so that they can have tax-free distributions and avoid mandatory withdrawals when they reach age 70 1/2. A Roth IRA makes sense if they have a good after-tax cash flow. Their first step should be to check what their current 401(k) contribution is and to estimate what tax bracket they will be in when they retire. If they expect to be in a lower tax bracket, then it is a better move to increase current 401(k) contributions in order to take the 28 percent deferral now. When they retire, they can take a 401(k) rollover to a traditional IRA then convert part of it to a Roth IRA. The conversion will be at a lower tax rate which will increase the value of their retirement portfolio.

Abigail is 30, in the 15 percent tax bracket, and her salary is expected to grow in the years to come. She has no company retirement plan but she does have enough after tax-cash flow to invest $2,000 into an IRA. Abigail would like to save more for retirement but the IRA is the only retirement investment available to her. She is eligible for both the Roth and the traditional, tax-deductible IRA.

In this case, Abigail is better off contributing to the Roth IRA. Because her tax bracket will likely be the same or higher when she retires, the $2,000 Roth IRA contribution will be worth more than the same size contribution to a traditional, tax-deferred IRA by the time taxes are paid on withdrawals.

Sandy is 30, in the 28 percent tax bracket, and has a 401(k) at work. She is thinking about cutting back on her 401(k) contributions in order to invest in a Roth IRA. This would be a very bad move. Sandy should take full advantage of the 28 percent tax deferral available from her 401(k) before looking at the Roth. It would take her $2,778 to get $2,000 into her Roth IRA because her contributions are taxed at 28 percent. It would be better for her to contribute the full $2,780 into her 401(k). Until she can afford to max out contributions to her 401(k), she shouldn't even look at a Roth.

You may have noticed by now that changing just one or two variables can make a big difference in which IRA to use. It is important to sit down, evaluate your entire portfolio, look at all the trade-offs, and then make a decision that best fits your unique situation.

Strategy If You Decide Not to Retire

Many individuals decide to work past the age that they could otherwise choose to retire. This decision may be based on the need for additional income, the need for medical coverage, or simply because they like the social interaction that a job provides. The Roth IRA really comes in handy in this situation because you can continue making contributions after age 70 1/2 without having to take minimum withdrawals. It is important, however, to start your Roth IRA early because it must exist for five years before you can start making qualified withdrawals. As long as you have enough after-tax cash flow, funding a Roth IRA makes a lot of sense in this situation. You may also consider converting a traditional IRA to a Roth IRA.

Strategy Once You Are Retired

Once you finally do retire, all the factors involved in retirement planning are known—but of course now its too late to do anything about it! You are no longer eligible for IRA contributions when you stop earning income as defined by the IRS. Even so, you can still include an IRA in your plans if you have funds in a qualified, pre-tax retirement plan that can be rolled into a new IRA. If you have a 401(k), a profit sharing plan, or a pension plan that allows lump sum distributions, then the rollover is an option you can consider.

Convert Or Not to Convert

The decision to contribute to a Roth IRA versus a traditional IRA is small in comparison to the decision of converting an existing IRA to a Roth IRA. A traditional IRA may be converted to a Roth IRA in any tax year. The pre-tax contributions converted to a Roth IRA are taxable in the year converted. An exception is made for conversions made in 1998 where the taxable amount is spread out over 4 years. Certain restrictions apply. See Roth IRA Chapter 3.

The advantages of converting a traditional IRA to a Roth IRA are that you are not required to take minimum withdrawals when you reach age 70 1/2 and you get tax-free distributions during your lifetime and at death. The disadvantage is that you will owe taxes on any tax-deferred money that is converted.

What Makes a Conversion Unattractive

- You will owe taxes on the taxable conversion in the year of conversion.

- It is not a good tax strategy to convert during a time when your tax bracket is higher than what you expect it to be when you make distributions.

What Makes a Conversion Attractive to Investors

- No minimum withdrawal required at age 70 1/2.
- Tax free distributions during lifetime and at death.
- It is a good tax strategy to convert during a time when your tax bracket is lower than what you expect it to be when you make distributions.

Caution

Be careful not to convert a sum that is large enough to push you into a higher tax bracket. Convert a portion of the IRA over several years until the desired accumulated amount is converted. Conversions performed in 1998 are spread over four years. You can effectively spread the conversion out over any period you desire by doing partial conversions each year.

- A conversion is very beneficial to young investors when their traditional IRA contains mostly after-tax contributions. This is because conversion taxes are not applied to after-tax contributions. They are only applied to investment earnings and tax-deductible contributions.

Things to Consider

- Conversion funds must be reported as income for that year. Be careful that the conversion does not push you into higher tax bracket.

- Avoid using funds from a retirement plan to pay for conversion taxes.

- Plan conversions to take advantage of tax rates.

- Be sure you have enough after-tax money to pay taxes on the conversion.

- In reality the conversion does not make sense for many individuals. Starting a Roth IRA is a good idea for many but converting may not be beneficial.

A substantial amount of taxes becomes due when a conversion is made. If a $100,000 IRA is converted and you are in the 28 percent marginal tax rate then you will owe $28,000 in taxes. The money converted must be reported as income for that year. This could easily push you into the next higher tax bracket causing you to pay more than 28 percent. Before converting to a Roth IRA, be sure that the increased return on your investment during retirement will overcome the taxes you must pay today.

It is not wise to pay taxes on the conversion with funds removed from the converted IRA. Use out-of-pocket money so that you don't reduce the value of the IRA. Assuming the same investment results, $100,000 in a Roth IRA is much more valuable than $100,000 in a traditional IRA. You can effectively increase the value of your IRA by converting to a Roth when paying taxes out of after-tax cash flow.

Many conditions must be taken into account when deciding whether or not to convert a traditional IRA to a Roth IRA. You must look at your current tax bracket and what you expect it to be when you retire, along with how much after-tax cash flow you have, what kind of retirement investments you already have, and how you will use IRA funds during retirement. Tax brackets and the use of IRA funds during retirement are the biggest factors to consider.

If you expect to be in a lower tax bracket during retirement then staying with the traditional IRA is a good choice. It will cost more to pay taxes on the conversion when you are in a higher tax bracket than to distribute the funds and pay taxes at a lower rate during retirement. On the other hand, if you expect to be in a higher tax bracket at retirement, converting to a Roth IRA can be beneficial. Taxes on the conversion will use your current tax bracket. When you jump to a higher tax bracket and make withdrawals they will be tax-free. If you expect to remain in the same tax bracket when you retire, you need to consider the additional factor of how your IRA funds will be used.

An early retirement or immediate start of distributions at retirement tends to favor the traditional IRA if the tax brackets are the same or lower. If you plan to retire before age 59 1/2 and want to use your IRA funds during this time, then the traditional IRA is more advantageous because you can access it using substantially equal payments (See Chapter 2). If you do not plan to use your IRA for a continual distribution to depletion during retirement then the Roth IRA is the best choice and a conversion may be a good idea. Remember that the power of a Roth IRA is its ability to continue tax-free accumulation without ever requiring minimum distributions.

You can increase the value of a conversion by carefully selecting how and when you do it. For example, let's say you are a couple of years from retirement and you have a $100,000 traditional IRA that you don't need to use right away. Converting to a Roth IRA is a good idea. Let's also say that you are currently in the 28 percent tax bracket and expect to drop down to a 15 percent bracket when you retire. You should wait until retirement before converting the IRA so that you will be in a lower tax bracket. You can also perform the conversion in parts over a few years so that you can keep your taxable income within your current tax bracket.

Converting When You Are Close to Retirement

Converting to a Roth IRA can be a very powerful strategy if you are close to retirement. It gives you the opportunity to off-load tax burdens now in order to avoid forced distributions and increased tax burdens later. Not only does this produce big tax savings, but it gives you the opportunity to build substantial wealth in the later years of your retirement. If you have access to income from company pensions, 401(k) plans, Social Security and personal income, then your IRA will not be the main source of your income. In this case, being able to continue IRA growth in the later years as these other income sources are depleted makes the Roth IRA conversion very appealing.

The more money you have in a traditional IRA and the longer the expected delay in using your funds the more beneficial it becomes to convert. An IRA worth $200,000 to $300,000 near retirement may grow to over $500,000 by the time minimum withdrawals are required from a traditional IRA. This can create a large tax burden. If, on the other hand, you expect to drop into a lower tax bracket at retirement and you plan to use your IRA money right away, then converting to a Roth IRA may not be beneficial. It doesn't make sense to pay conversion taxes at your higher tax bracket and then get tax-free distributions at your lower tax rate.

Table 5.2 shows the difference in outcomes if an investor converts an existing IRA to a Roth or leaves the IRA pre-tax. It shows what the outcome would be if you converted a $100,000 traditional IRA to a Roth IRA five years before retirement and paid $28,000 in conversion taxes ($7,000 per year for four years). It then shows four additional cases where the money is left in the traditional IRA and the $28,000 that would have otherwise been spent on conversion taxes is invested either pre-tax or after-tax in chunks of $7,000 per year for four years. The example assumes the investor is close to retirement and will start distributions at retirement. Look at the last column, "Total After-Tax Distribution" for the bottom line. Case 1 and Case 2 show that if you remain in the 28 percent tax bracket when you retire, the conversion is a good choice

Table 5.2 Convert vs. Don't Convert

Account Type	Taxable amount on Conversion	Tax rate at Retirement	Value at distribution	Yearly after-tax distribution	Total after-tax distribution
Roth	Paid to IRS	n/a	$ 157,351.94	$ 13,502.45	$ 337,561.25
Case 1	Invested pre-tax	28%	$ 209,393.51	$12,937.05	$ 323,426.25
Case 2	Invested after-tax	28%	$ 191,945.45	$12,186.10	$ 304,652.50
Case 3	Invested pre-tax	15%	$ 209,393.51	$15,272.90	$ 381,822.50
Case 4	Invested after-tax	15%	$ 191,945.45	$ 14,157.58	$ 353,939.50

The first line in this table shows what you get if you convert a $100,000 traditional IRA to a Roth IRA five years before retirement. Taxes due on this conversion equal $28,000 payable at $7,000 per year for four years. The scenarios illustrated in Cases 1-4 show what happens if you leave the money in the traditional IRA and invest the $28,000 in chunks of $7,000 per year in either a pre-tax or an after-tax investment at a rate of 12 percent. Pre-retirement taxes are assumed to be 28 percent. Retirement taxes are analyzed at both the 28 percent and the 15 percent rate. Retirement distributions are for 25 years at a 7 percent investment return. Look at the last column, "Total After-Tax Distribution" for the bottom line. Case 1 and Case 2 show that if you remain in the 28 percent tax bracket when you retire, the conversion is a good choice whether you use the money in the early or late part of your retirement. If, on the other hand, your tax bracket drops to 15 percent when you retire, the conversion is not the best choice. Keep in mind that this example is for a very specific set of conditions.

whether you use the money in the early or late part of your retirement. If, on the other hand, your tax bracket drops to 15 percent when you retire, the conversion is not the best choice.

TIP: A big factor when evaluating whether or not to convert a traditional IRA to a Roth IRA is whether or not you have enough after-tax cash flow to pay the conversion taxes. You should also examine your portfolio to determine if you are taking full advantage of all pre-tax investment opportunities (i.e. your 401(k) plan if one is available). Analyses intended to show whether or not a conversion is desirable often assume the money that would otherwise be used to pay conversion taxes is invested in a taxable account. These analyses do not show what would happen if you invested the money in a nontaxable account. As you can see from Table 5.2, this consideration can make a big difference so be sure to include it in your own analysis.

Joe & Diane are 60 and plan to retire in three years. They expect to have adequate income generated from a company pension, Social Security and personal savings to fund their retirement. They are currently in the 28 percent tax bracket but will drop into the 15 percent bracket at retirement. They have about $100,000 in a traditional IRA that they do not plan to use. Joe and Diane decide to convert to a Roth IRA. The amount of taxes due on the conversion is $28,000.

Evaluating the Roth IRA

The further you are from retirement, the more difficult it is to evaluate a Roth conversion because you cannot accurately predict all the variables involved. In addition, during the early years your after-tax cash flow is not usually large enough to cover conversion taxes.

If they convert in 1998 they can spread the taxes due over four years and pay $7,000 per year for a total of $28,000. On the other hand, if they wait until retirement they can convert the entire IRA at the 15 percent rate. In addition, if they convert only $20,000 per year for five years they will only have to pay $3,000 per year for a total of $15,000. This is a $13,000 tax savings— good move! Of course the $100,000 IRA will continue to grow in the three years until they retire and it will continue to grow during the five year conversion period. What to do with this excess money? It can be converted, left in the traditional IRA as pre-tax money, or withdrawn. The after-tax cash flow funds they would save by not converting during the three working years can be invested in a money market fund and used to pay conversion taxes during retirement. The disadvantage of not converting the excess funds right away is that a Roth IRA cannot be distributed tax-free until it is five years old. Since Joe and Diane are not planning to use the money right away, waiting five years is not a problem. You can see that a little bit of planning can reap huge rewards.

Karen & Bob are 60 and plan to retire in three to four years. They expect to have adequate income generated from a company pension, Social Security and personal savings to fund their retirement. They are currently in the 28 percent tax bracket and will remain in the 28 percent tax bracket during retirement. They have a $100,000 IRA they do not plan to use right away and they want to convert it. Their MAGI is below $100,000 and they have enough cash flow to cover conversion taxes. Since they do not plan to use the funds and do not want to have forced distributions at age 70 1/2 a conversion is a good move. The biggest concern is to make the conversion without pushing their income into a higher tax bracket. A conversion in 1998 requires a four year spread of taxes. After 1998, partial conversions can be made over the span of a few years to control taxable income in any given year. In this case, it is a good idea to convert as soon as possible so that the Roth IRA can begin growing tax free. It also

---

Evaluating a Roth Conversion

Mathematically, a Roth conversion is beneficial for investors who accumulate large portfolios and end up in a higher tax bracket during retirement. It is also good for those who do not need to use their IRA funds during retirement. If you intend to retire and use your IRA funds before age 59 1/2 or during the early years of your retirement, then the traditional IRA may be more advantageous. In some cases it is very easy to rationalize whether or not to convert IRA funds to a Roth IRA, but most cases can be argued either way based on many assumptions.

gives them a head start on the five year wait period.

John is 35 years old and has accumulated $60,000 in an IRA. He is currently in the 15 percent tax bracket but future salary raises and promotions will move him into the 28 percent bracket. He saves 10 percent of his salary in the company 401(k) and makes a $2,000 nondeductible annual contribution to a traditional IRA. Since John will soon be in the 28 percent tax bracket, a conversion should be made now if he wishes to do so. After looking at all his investments, John decides to convert the $60,000 IRA to a Roth IRA while he is in the 15 percent tax bracket. He will have a sizable 401(k) by retirement and feels the Roth will give him flexibility with distributions. He also expects to be in the 28 percent bracket at retirement which also makes the conversion a good idea. To convert a $60,000 IRA while in the 15 percent tax bracket a total of $9,000 is due in taxes. This assumes all funds are pre-tax. John does the conversion in 1998 which means he will pay the taxes over the next four years. If his salary increases, he may be in the 28 percent tax bracket by the fourth year. This will require a higher tax payment on the final conversion amount. Another strategy John implements is to redirect his $2,000 nondeductible annual contribution from a traditional IRA to his new Roth IRA.

John actually has a portion of funds in his $60,000 IRA that are not taxable when converted because his contributions were made with after-tax money. Let's assume that $15,000 of the $60,000 is after-tax money. When the $60,000 is converted to a Roth only $45,000 has a tax liability. This means a total of $6,750 will be due in taxes over the next four years. The $15,000 will now accumulate tax-free rather than tax-deferred. This is a very good move for investors who have nondeductible funds in a IRA.

Bill and Cindy are married, in their thirties and have large account values in their 401(k) plans. The size of their IRA's is small and they contain about half pre-tax money and half after-tax money due to nondeductible contributions. They want to start a Roth IRA in order to supplement their 401(k) investment. The IRA's are worth $20,000 all together with $10,000 being after-tax money. Bill and Cindy are in the 28 percent tax bracket and will owe $2,800 in conversion taxes. Since they can convert in 1998 and pay $700 in taxes per year for four years they choose this option. The conversion will give them $20,000 in Roth IRA's in 1998. They can contribute to their new Roth IRA's and accumulate tax free wealth as long as they want.

Converting to a Roth IRA can be beneficial for young investors who have a significant amount of after-tax contributions in their traditional IRA. Since conversion taxes are not applied to the after-tax portion of the IRA, the tax liability may not be too burdensome. Conversion taxes are applied to past earnings and to tax-deductible contributions. By converting after-tax contributions from a traditional IRA to a Roth IRA, you gain the benefit of tax-free growth on earnings. If the money remains in a traditional IRA, earnings are tax-deferred which means taxes are due when distributions are made.

There is no magic formula that says a conversion is beneficial if x percent of the traditional IRA contains after-tax contributions and y percent contains pre-tax contributions. The larger the percent of after-tax contributions, the better a conversion looks. Don't just look at the ratio of pre-tax contributions to after-tax contributions. Make sure you look at the dollar amount of taxes due on the conversion. You don't want investment momentum to be reduced by the affect of a big tax burden. It is also important to note that when you convert an IRA with after-tax funds, you cannot convert just the after-tax portion. You must convert a ratio based on your after-tax basis as determined by IRS form 8606.

NOTE: IRS guidance recommends that trustees set up conversion Roth's separately from contribution IRA's for accounting purposes. When Bill and Cindy convert their IRA it will be placed in a conversion IRA. They will then each set up a contribution IRA.

Sally and Sterling are 35 years old, married and have a combined $200,000 in IRA's from previous rollovers and investments. All the funds are pre-tax. They are in the 28 percent tax bracket and invest in their company 401(k). They do not contribute to an IRA. Their AGI is less than $100,000. They will rely mainly on their 401(k) and IRA for retirement funding. Their after-tax cash flow is good. Should they convert all or some of their IRA? It is very possible that they will accumulate a substantial sum in their retirement accounts and will stay in the 28 percent bracket. If they convert their existing IRA's to a Roth they will pay $56,000 in taxes. This is a substantial drain on current cash flow. A good strategy is to leave the IRA's alone and contribute $2,000 each for a total of $4,000 per year to a Roth IRA with their after-tax cash flow. This will enable them to build up a sizable Roth IRA of over $500,000 during their remaining investment years. The traditional IRA's can be used to fund early retirement while the Roth continues to grow. The idea is to avoid losing momentum on retirement investments by paying out large sums of money in taxes. It is a better idea to use money that would otherwise pay conversion taxes to continue investing.

Jack and Jill are also 35 years old, married and have a combined $200,000 in IRA's from previous rollovers and investments. They are in the 28 percent tax bracket and invest in their company 401(k). Unlike the above example they contribute to a Roth IRA. Their AGI is less than $100,000. They will rely mainly on their 401(k) and IRA for retirement funding. They have excellent after-tax cash flow and wish to contribute more towards retirement. They think they will be in at least a 28 percent tax bracket during retirement and expect to have more income than they need from their 401(k)'s and IRA's. Their incomes are increasing and will eventually exceed the Roth conversion AGI of $100,000. Should they convert all or some of their IRA? In this case, a partial conversion can be beneficial. Since they are well on their way to building a retirement vehicle that will produce an excess of what they need in the early part of retirement a partial conversion will help them diversify their tax liabilities. This case is difficult to predict since the couple is so far from retirement. Variables such as retirement tax bracket, retirement age, and income needs are difficult to predict when retirement is so far away.

NOTE: There are many gray areas when it comes to converting to a Roth IRA for younger individuals with large 401(k)'s. The above scenarios are the basic cases. You can argue it either way. One intangible to consider is you have the funds deferred. It will cost you money to convert. The money leaves your portfolio today. When you are looking at 20 to 30 years to retirement, giving up money is a tough call. You are trying to gauge if it is better to have a tax liability on a large portfolio or no tax on a small portfolio. It is almost a coin toss! I like keeping and investing the money now and settling with Uncle Sam later. This, coupled with contributing into a Roth IRA, is a very good strategic plan for young individuals in higher tax brackets who have large IRA's invested for retirement.

Borrowing from Retirement Vehicles

One of the most common questions asked is whether or not to borrow from a retirement vehicle. The basic answer is no. Tax deferral works best if you let your money compound at a higher rate over a long time period. By borrowing or removing funds from your account, you lose investment opportunities. This rational assumes you have a good debt management plan outside of your retirement investments. If you are paying 21 percent on credit cards and other consumer loans, then earning 15 percent in equities in your retirement plan is not getting you anywhere—at least not upwards!

The new IRA encourages use as a short-term savings vehicle. This is a good opportunity for some investors but it may cause others to fall short on long-term retirement needs. Make sure your retirement needs are funded before you use a retirement account to provide for short-term desires.

Chapter 6

What You Need to Know About Investing

If you want to be a successful IRA investor, start with a good overall strategy, select investments that will carry out your strategy and implement your decisions. Poor strategy, selection or implementation can quickly defeat the advantages of IRA investing. You learned how to create a good strategy in the last chapter. Now its time to talk about investment selection and implementation.

The object is to select investments for your IRA that will maximize the benefits of tax deferral. For example, it doesn't make sense to use tax-exempt bonds because they are tax-favored on their own. If you put them in a traditional IRA, you will actually lose ground because the gains will be taxed at distribution. Not only that, but tax-exempt bonds have a low return so you won't be taking advantage of the tax-deferred compounding opportunity that an IRA offers. In the same manner, money market funds are not suitable inside an IRA. Their returns are too low. A money market gives you stability of principle so that you can have access to funds quickly in the short term. If you put a money market in your IRA you're money is tied up until retirement and you defeat the whole purpose. If you want to manage taxes related to your money market funds, use a tax-exempt money market outside your

IRA. A variable or fixed annuity is another poor choice for your IRA. The tax advantages are redundant and the variable or fixed annuity product is very expensive. It carries high hidden fees that will eat away at the tax-deferred features of an IRA.

Investments that benefit most from an IRA are the ones that produce the largest gains. Outside the IRA, these investments are taxed, so you lose money. Inside an IRA, gains are sheltered from taxes which gives you more money to work with. In addition, large gains are needed to take full advantage of the tax-deferred compounding available in an IRA. Equities and high yielding bonds usually have the high returns that perform well inside an IRA. Take a look at the historical returns of stocks (S&P 500 benchmark) as compared to bonds (LBB benchmark) and Treasury Bills as shown in Table 6.1. You can see that stocks have a much higher return.

Minimize Investment Cost

Cost management is an important part of investing. Fees and expenses must be managed just like in any other business. The goal is to get the most value out of the cost you incur to invest.

A good investment strategy can be defeated by expenses. Look carefully at account fees, wrap fees, sales loads, and transaction fees. It is your mission to uncover hidden costs. It is the investment industry's strategy to hide them!

Seek Investments that Fit Your Risk and Return Profile

While the proper selection of mutual funds and stocks is important for long-term investment success, it is not within the scope of this book to cover this area. To get you started, however, take a look at Table 6.1 containing benchmark returns. Use these values to compare returns of funds you are looking at. A good fund will have returns greater than it's

Table 6.1 Benchmark Returns

Fund Category	1997	1996	1995	1994	1993	1992	1991	1990	1989	1988	3 YR	5 YR	10 YR
S&P 500	33.35	22.95	37.53	1.31	10.06	7.7	30.33	-3.11	31.59	16.5	31.13%	20.25%	18.02%
Russell 2000	22.37	16.54	28.44	-1.82	18.91	18.41	46.05	-19.5	16.25	24.9	22.35%	16.42%	15.76%
LBB Aggregate	9.68	3.61	18.47	-2.92	9.75	7.24	16	8.94	14.59	7.87	10.42%	7.48%	9.16%
MSCI EAFE	1.78	6.05	11.21	7.78	32.56	-12.17	12.13	-23.45	10.54	28.27	6.28%	11.39%	6.25%
MSCI World	15.76	13.48	20.72	5.08	22.50	-5.22	18.28	-17.12	16.6	23.29	16.61%	15.34%	10.55%
T-Bills	5.07	5.00	5.51	4.27	3.02	3.46	5.41	7.51	8.11	6.67	5.20%	4.59%	5.42%

Use this table to compare the performance of your mutual funds. The S&P 500 is your equity fund benchmark. The Russell 2000 is used as a benchmark for small stocks. The LBB Aggregate (Lehman Brothers Bond Aggregate) is a bond fund benchmark. The MSCI EAFE is used to measure the overall foreign market movement. The MSCI World is a world market equity fund.

benchmark. Stay away from funds that underperform their benchmarks. Table 6.2 lists several funds that are excellent performers in their categories.

Implement Your Investment Selections

Almost any mutual fund company will allow you to invest in their funds via an IRA. The exception is the educational IRA. It will probably be difficult to find a worthy mutual fund to invest in directly because the Educational IRA does not involve much money. Traditional and Roth IRA's can be established for less than the minimum starting amount typically required for most mutual funds. For example, the minimum initial investment for the Vanguard Index 500 is $3,000 but for an IRA it is $1,000. There are many funds that allow you to

Table 6.2 Top Performing Mutual Funds

Investment Objective	Fund Name	Investment Style
Worldwide	Janus Worldwide	Large growth stocks
Worldwide	Tweedy Brown Global Value	Medium value Stocks
Growth	Oakmark	Medium to large value stocks
Growth	Tweedy Brown American Value	Medium value stocks
Growth	T-Rove Price Mid-Cap Growth	Medium growth stocks
Growth & Income	T-Rowe Price Equity-Income	Large value stocks
Growth & Income	Vanguard Index 500	large mix of value and growth stocks
Small Stock	Fidelity Low Price Stock	Small value and growth stocks

Use this table as a quick start to finding mutual funds that are top performers in their categories

Table 6.3 Fund Company Phone Numbers

Fund Company	Phone Number
American Century	1-800-345-2021
Dodge & Cox	1-800-621-3979
Fidelity Funds	1-800-544-8888
Janus Funds	1-800-525-8983
Oakmark Funds	1-800-625-6275
T. Rowe Price	1-800-638-5660
Tweedy Brown	1-800-432-4789
Vanguard Group	1-800-662-7447

This table lists several fund companies that allow direct access to their funds.

establish an IRA with as little as $500.

Some very good no-load and low load mutual fund companies that allow you to access their funds directly are listed in Table 6.3.

With the exception of Fidelity, the fund companies listed above are completely no-load. Fidelity has a mix of no-load and low-load funds that may be accessed directly. Many of the low-load funds waive the load for IRA investors. Fidelity funds sold via a broker are usually full-load funds from the Fidelity Advisor series. There are many no-load fund families available that offer good funds. Our list is limited due to space.

Superstar funds can be found in some fund families and each fund has its own style and objective. You won't find a single fund family that has superstar funds covering every style and objective. In fact, some fund families don't have any funds that are worth investing in at all! When choosing a mutual fund, start by determining your asset allocation and investment objective needs then find a top performing fund that meets these requirements.

Vanguard funds specialize in index type funds. They have a group of outstanding index funds that cover almost any type of index you could want. Their flagship fund is the S&P 500 index fund. It is by far the industry leader and is an excellent equity fund to have in your portfolio. T-Rowe Price offers many good funds in different investment objectives. Oakmark is a value style investment company that has several outstanding funds. Fidelity, the industry leader, has many excellent domestic stock funds. Their foreign funds, however, have not provided returns that live up to the reputation built on domestic funds.

You can typically have as many funds from one fund family as you want as long as you meet whatever the required minimum for that fund company is. If you have a lot of money in your IRA, its a good idea to spread it across several different mutual funds. This gives you diversity in risk and return and it will strengthen your portfolio. If you want several funds that all fall under different fund families, you will need to establish a separate IRA with each company.

Suppose you have established an IRA with Oakmark and decide you would like to contribute some of your future contributions to the Tweedy Brown Value Fund. You would then need to establish an IRA fund with Tweedy Brown. You can have as many IRA's as you want. The only limitation is that your annual contribution is limited to $2,000. A qualified rollover is not restricted by the $2,000 limit. If you want to invest in three different funds with different fund families you would establish an IRA with each of them. Of course you must satisfy any initial minimum for establishing the IRA as well as minimums for subsequent additional contributions. Don't take on too many IRA's that require a trustee fee which can impede your overall portfolio value.

Another way to invest in several fund families with one IRA is to use a discount broker. You can establish one IRA with a discount broker and invest in multiple no-load funds from different fund families. Many discount brokers offer a no-load, no transaction fee network of funds. These funds may

Table 6.4 Discount Broker Phone Numbers

Discount Broker	Phone Number
Waterhouse Securities	1-800-934-4410
Schwab	1-800-435-4000
Jack White & Co.	1-800-753-1700
Fidelity Brokerage	1-800-544-7272

This table lists several discount brokers that have a no-load, no-transaction fee network

be accessed without fees. Major discount brokers that have a no-load, no-transaction fee network are listed in Table 6.4.

Let's say you have $100,000 in a 401(k) plan and want to roll the money into an IRA that invests in three different mutual funds from three different fund families. The three funds are Oakmark Fund, Vanguard Index 500, and Fidelity Low Priced Stock Fund. There are several ways to implement this strategy. You could establish a separate IRA with each of the three companies. You could use a discount broker who offers all three funds in a mutual fund network. You could also use a combination approach where you set up an IRA with a discount broker and another IRA directly with a mutual fund company.

A 401(k) company direct agent transfer can be made to each agent all at one time. This allows you to transfer one-third of your portfolio directly to each of the three fund families. Your employer, however, may only want to transfer directly to one agent or they may want to give the money directly to you via a *rollover to you*. Do not choose the *rollover to you* method because you will have 20 percent in taxes withheld for Uncle Sam. Instead, you can use a *direct agent transfer* to one mutual fund company then transfer money to the other fund companies.

Paul has a $100,000 401(k) plan from a previous company. He wants to roll it over into an IRA and invest his IRA equally in three different funds. His previous employer will not direct transfer to multiple agents. They offer to send the rollover funds directly to him so he can cash the check and distribute the money himself. They tell him the funds will have 20 percent removed and sent to the IRS. To avoid this, Paul decides to have the entire direct agent transfer go to the Vanguard mutual fund company to be placed in a money market fund. From here he immediately sets up and transfers one-third of the money into the Oakmark Fund and one-third into Fidelity's Low Priced Stock Fund. After the transfer, he then moves the funds from the money market into the S&P 500 index fund at Vanguard. This strategy allows Paul to perform a direct agent transfer and establish the investment selection he wants without cost or tax withholding hassles. If Paul's funds where already in an IRA he could just transfer funds to another fund company as he desired.

Another approach is to have the rollover sent directly to a discount broker. From here the money can be invested in the funds of several different fund companies. This strategy offers convenience of a single IRA location. Many discount brokers offer no-load funds in a no transaction fee network. Be sure the funds you want are in the no transaction fee network. If not, you will pay a transaction fee. There may also be load funds in the network. You will then be subject to a load as well. Another advantage of discount brokers is that you can invest in individual stocks and bonds from the same IRA. Discount brokers offer convenience and reasonable pricing. Major discount brokers that provide no-load fund networks include Waterhouse, Jack White and Company, Charles Schwab, Fidelity, Vanguard, and T-Rowe Price.

Using a combination of discount broker and investing directly with a fund family is a good way to access different funds at the lowest cost. For instance, Oakmark Growth Funds can be entered by a no transaction fee with several discount brokers. The Vanguard 500 Index fund, however, will incur a transaction fee. You could establish an IRA directly with the fund families that are not available through a discount broker without transaction fees and still use the discount broker for funds that are in the no-load, no transaction fee network. The discount broker will also give you access to individual securities. Be aware that different discount brokers will have a different set of no-load, no-transaction fees.

With so many different types of IRA's it will be common for investors to have more than one You could easily have a traditional IRA, a Roth IRA, a Roth conversion IRA and a traditional conduit IRA. Don't be afraid to have multiple IRA's. Just remember to find the best investments that fit your situation, manage cost and fees then let the number of IRA's fall where they may.

The *Investor's Resource Guide* contains a wealth of information to help you find names and numbers of most of the no-load funds and discount brokers (see end of book for ordering information). Information on data and statistics is included to help you in your selection. You will also finds tips to help guide you in the maze of data and funds available.

All About the New IRA

Chapter 7

All About the SEP and SARSEP IRA

The Self-Employed Pension, or **SEP**, was created by the Revenue Act of 1978. It provides a low cost, easy-to-set-up and easy-to-maintain retirement plan for small businesses and for self-employed individuals. It is just like an IRA in the way it is created and maintained. You will often hear it referred to as a SEP-IRA. The SEP is created for the employee but the employer makes the contributions. The advantage of a SEP is that you can make larger contributions than you can in a traditional IRA.

Your employer can contribute up to 15 percent of your salary or up to $30,000, whichever is less. Because contributions are made by the employer, it is the employer who benefits from tax-deductible contributions. However, contributions are not reported as income on your W-2 form. Employers do not have to make contributions each year. When contributions are made they must be made for each eligible employee. Eligibility is typically limited to any employee who is over 21 years of age, has been employed for at least three of the preceding five years, and who has received at least $400 in compensation from the employer for that tax year. An employer may establish less restrictive eligibility requirements if they desire. They may not, however, impose limits that are more restrictive.

The SEP is considered a defined-contribution plan. If you have more than one defined-contribution plan, the total of all contributions cannot exceed the lesser of $30,000 or 25 percent of earnings.

You may make contributions to your SEP in addition to the contributions made by your employer. The amount you can contribute is limited by the same restrictions as those imposed on the traditional IRA. You can contribute up to $2,000 per year. The contribution may or may not be deductible depending on your IRA eligibility. You must claim all deductible contributions on your 1040 form. Nondeductible earnings should be claimed using IRS form 8606.

If you are self-employed or you are operating as a partnership, you may use line 28 of form 1040 to take a deduction for any employer contributions to your SEP-IRA. If you make additional contributions as an individual, you may use line 23 of form 1040 to take your own deduction. Remember that your income and filing status determine what you are eligible to contribute on a tax-deductible basis.

Once employer contributions are made to the SEP-IRA, they belong to the employee. An employer can not prohibit withdrawals or place restrictions on the money. This means you are 100 percent vested immediately in your SEP-IRA company retirement plan. Contributions made by the employer are pre-tax to the participant. Distributions from a SEP-IRA follow the traditional IRA rules.

A special feature of the SEP-IRA allows the company to set up a Salary Reduction SEP—also known as a SARSEP. The Salary Reduction Simplified Employee Pension-Individual Retirement Account, or **SARSEP-IRA** enables employees to defer part of their salary into the plan. The employer deposits wages pre-tax into the SARSEP IRA for the employee. The employee defers taxes on the earned income. This is similar to the popular 401(k) plan.

The SARSEP allows employee deferrals of up to 15 percent of compensation or $9,500. This is significantly higher than a traditional IRA. Salary deferrals are included in your wages for Social Security and Medicare taxes. They are not included in wages for federal income taxes. This is similar to

401(k) deferrals.

SARSEP-IRA's are no longer allowed to be established. This type of plan was phased out by the 1996 tax changes. An existing plan may continue to operate. The SARSEP was replaced with the Savings Incentive Match Plan for Employees (**SIMPLE**). The SIMPLE plan may be set up using IRA's or as a 401(k).

The SIMPLE IRA plan uses an IRA for each participant. An employee may defer part of their salary into the IRA. The employer must either match the contribution or make nonelective contributions as required by plan rules. No other types of contributions may be made to the plan.

To be eligible for the SIMPLE IRA, employers typically must have fewer than 100 employees and they may not maintain any other active retirement plan. One of two types of employee contributions must be made to employees and the employee must be given a 60 day period to make elections or changes to their arrangement.

The maximum an employee may defer is $6,000 per year. The amount is indexed for inflation in $500 increments. The deferral amount is expressed as a percentage of salary by the plan document. An employee may not be able to contribute the maximum dollars if the plan's defined percentage of salary is more restrictive.

The employer must either match the employee's contribution dollar-for-dollar, up to 3 percent, or make a 2 percent of salary contribution to all eligible employees whether or not they contribute to the plan.

If the employer chooses to make matching contributions, then the 3 percent match is required for all employees contributing at least 3 percent of their salary. An employer may elect a lesser match as low as 1 percent. This is to help employers navigate difficult economic times. A percentage less than 3 percent can not be in place more than 2 years in any five year period. If a lower match is elected the employer must notify each participant prior to the 60 day election period. This allows each employee the opportunity to change their deferrals based on the lower match.

An employer may chose to make a 2 percent, nonelective contribution on behalf of all eligible employees instead of the match. Basically, every employee who qualifies to participate in the plan, even if they don't choose to do so, must receive the contribution if the matching option is not chosen. Employees must be notified the 2 percent contribution option was elected prior to their 60 day election period.

Employee contributions must be placed into the SIMPLE accounts within 30 days after the end of the month in which wages to the employee were deferred. Employer contributions must be made by the due date for filing the employer's income tax return for the year.

Distributions from the SIMPLE plan are subject to IRA rules. An early withdrawal in the first two years of participation is subject to a 25 percent penalty. This is higher than the 10 percent penalty on other plans. The 10 percent penalty is in affect for early withdrawals after the first two years.

The SIMPLE IRA is an outstanding retirement plan for many small business owners and employees. If you are an employee, be sure to take advantage of this opportunity. If your employer does not have a retirement plan let them know about this one. It is relatively cheap. The money the employer must dedicate to contributions is typically recovered by the savings that would be required to set up and administer a 401(k) or other retirement plan.

Investment principles used with a SEP, SARSEP or SIMPLE plan are all the same. The idea is to take advantage of tax deferral. Investment selection is the same as for any other tax-deferred retirement plan such as a 401(k) or traditional IRA.

Participants typically have flexibility to where they may establish their IRA. If you do not like the current investment selection, then transfer your IRA to a better investment opportunity. Be careful of any penalties or fees that may be triggered.

A P P E N D I X   A

How Taxes Affect Your Investment

As an investor, you need to have a basic understanding of how
the tax structure works because you only get to keep the after-
tax portion of your investment returns. Our government has
made it very difficult to calculate tax liabilities. There is no
way to discuss every aspect of taxation in this book. Fortunately, you do not need to be a tax expert. You do, however,
need to know what your personal tax situation is. You may
want to pull out the last few copies of your 1040 and W2 forms
and refer to them as we go along.

Let's take a look at the personal income tax structure and
how it relates to investing. Figure A-1 shows an overview of
how our income is taxed and how we are able to defer taxes.
The top block represents all income received in the tax year. It
includes earned income, investment or rental income, bonuses,
and certain other types of income.

If you have deferred income, it is subtracted from all
income received and not reported on line 22 of your 1040 form.
Line 22 represents all income received less deferred income.
Deferred income comes from pre-tax contributions into a
401(k) plan or other qualified retirement plan. It can also come
from deferred investment gains inside a qualified retirement
plan, IRA or Annuity.

The next step is to subtract out adjustments to your income.
This can be done if you are eligible for deductible contributions
to an IRA or Keogh plan. The result is your Adjusted Gross
Income (AGI) which further reduces your reported income.
The AGI is often referred to when talking about taxes or
investments. As you can see, it may be significantly lower
than the actual income you received in a given tax year.

Suppose you earn $30,000 a year working for a company
that has a 401(k) plan. If $30,000 is the entire amount of

Figure A-1 Tax Structure Diagram

All Income Received
Income reported on W2, K1, 1099R, 1099D. Also, income received as rental income, casual labor, and professional services.

Less Deferred Income	Reported Income
Elective Deferrals, 401(k), 403(b), SAR-SEP *W-2 Form Box 13&15*	Non-Deferred earned income, tips and other wages, bonuses, investment income, IRA and Pension Distributions *Form 1040 line 22 total income*

Adjustments to Income	Adjusted Gross Income (AGI)
IRA Deduction, Keogh Deduction, Moving Expenses *Form 1040 line 31*	Reported income less adjustments *Form 1040 line 32*

Deductions	Taxable Income
Itemized mortgage, medical expenses, charity, miscellaneous	AGI less deductions. This is the amount of money you pay taxes on. This number determines your marginal tax bracket. *Form 1040 line 38*

This diagram shows how your taxable income is calculated. You can reduce your taxable income to less than total income earned by deferring a portion of your income and by subtracting out qualified adjustments. If you are retired your income comes from investment returns and pension distributions. In this case, you must make quarterly estimated tax payments. If you are still working, then the taxes you owe are collected by withholding earnings.

income you received that year, and you choose not to defer any income, then your AGI is $30,000. Now, suppose your company allows you to defer up to 12 percent of your income into your 401(k) and you make a total annual contribution of $3,600. You now have $30,000 of income less $3,600 of deferred income which gives you an AGI of $26,400. If your AGI is within certain levels, you may make a tax deductible IRA contribution. This amount is recorded on line 23 and will lower your AGI.

To get to your final taxable income, you need to subtract out any qualified deductions that you are entitled to. Qualified deductions include such things as mortgage interest, real estate taxes and, charitable contributions.

As you can see, the amount you are subject to as taxable income can be far less than what you received as annual income. Tax deferment is a great way to build wealth. It allows you to borrow money from Uncle Sam so that you can invest it on your own behalf. With compound interest, this loan can be leveraged into a large sum of money. You will pay taxes on the distributions when you retire but the value of your account will be significantly larger than if the money had been invested in a taxable account.

Now you can see why tax deferment is considered such a good friend of investors. Just be very careful not to get so caught up with tax avoidance that you fail to see whether or not the investment opportunity is worthwhile. In other words, you may be able to find an investment yielding a higher return even though it is taxable.

In order to make good tax deferral investment choices you should understand where you stand with your ability to lower your taxable income and which marginal tax bracket you are in. Understanding the marginal tax bracket system is essential to making investment decisions.

How the Marginal Tax Rate System Works

You are probably familiar with the IRS tax brackets. Many working professionals are in the 28 percent tax bracket. This does not mean you pay 28 percent of your gross income in taxes. You actually pay less than that. Instead, 28 percent is the marginal tax rate at which the last incremental dollars of your income is taxed. This is important to understand because investment returns are typically taxed at the marginal rate.

To better understand the marginal tax rate system lets look at an example. This example is very general and is only intended to show the affect of the marginal tax rate.

Mr. & Mrs. Investor have a family earned income of $60,000 a year. They file as married filing jointly. For this example we will say that earned income is the same as AGI. Their personal exemptions of $7,950 (3 x $2,650 for 1997 tax filers) plus mortgage interest and property taxes of $7,000 allow them to deduct a total of $14,950 from their adjusted gross income. This leaves them with a taxable income of $45,050 ($60,000 - $14,950). You can now use the tax schedule to calculate their tax liability.

Many tax filers use the pre-calculated tables supplied by the IRS. The tax owed is already calculated using the formula and put into tables at $50 increments.

Use 1997 Schedule Y-1 (see Table A-1), married filing jointly, to calculate the taxes owed by Mr. & Mrs. Investor. For a taxable income between $41,200 and $99,600 the tax is $6,180 plus 28 percent of the amount over $41,200. Any taxable income over $41,200 is taxed at the next marginal rate.

In this example, the taxable income is over $41,200. We have an amount of $45,050 - $41,200 = $3,850 taxable at 28 percent.

Mr. & Mrs. Investor pay a lower rate of 15 percent on the first $41,200 of taxable income $6,180 / 41,200 = 0.15.

Table A-1   1997 Schedule Y-1

If the amount on Form 1040 line 38 is over	but not over	Enter on Form 1040 line 39	of the amount over...
$0	$41,200	15%	$0
$41,200	$99,600	$6180.00 + 28%	$41,200
$99,600	$151,750	$22,532.00 + 31%	$99,600
$151,750	$271,050	$38,698.50 + 36%	$151,750
$271,050	——	$81,646.50 + 39.6	$271,050

Use Schedule Y-1 if your filing status is Married Filing Jointly or Qualifying Widow(er).

Taxes owed on 28 percent marginal rate dollars = $3,850 x 28 percent = $1,078.

Their total tax liability is ($6,180 + $1,078) = $7,258.

They only paid 12.1 percent ($7,258 / $60,000 = 0.121) of earned income in taxes. They paid 16.1 percent ($7,258 / $45,050 = 0.161) of taxable income in taxes. This is because the first $41,200 of taxable income is taxed at the 15 percent rate. The remaining amount was taxed at 28 percent.

If their income rose $2,000 to $62,000, then they would pay taxes at the 28 percent rate on the $2,000 dollars which would be another $560 in taxes. This would increase their taxable income from $45,050 to $47,050 and their percent of taxes to 16.6 percent.

As you can see, for each additional dollar earned you pay taxes at the 28 percent rate. This is what is referred to as the marginal tax rate. It is the rate you pay for each additional dollar earned. Keep this idea in mind as you make investment decisions. If you can defer paying 28 percent of a portion of your earned or investment income in taxes you have found a powerful wealth building tool.

Two excellent tax-deferred investments are your company 401(k) plan and Individual Retirement Arrangements (IRA). Both of these investments allow you to defer some of your salary and they give you a tax break by lowering your taxable income. There are, of course, limitations to how much you can defer in these vehicles.

What Does MAGI (Modified Adjusted Gross Income) Mean?

Your MAGI (Modified Adjusted Gross Income) is used to calculate your IRA deductible eligibility. It is your Adjusted Gross Income (AGI) with certain deductions added back in. Depending on which form you use, 1040 or 1040A, the following items are added to your AGI in order to calculate your MAGI.

(1) IRA deduction

(2) Foreign Earned Income Exclusion

(3) Foreign housing exclusion or deduction

(4) Exclusion of series EE bond interest shown on form 8815 or exclusion of employer paid adoption expenses shown on form 8839

Use the worksheet provided with IRS form 1040 and IRS form 1040A to determine your IRA deduction eligibility.

A P P E N D I X   B

IRS Tax Forms

Form 1099-R
Distributions from Qualified Retirement Plans
Used by trustee to identify withdrawals from account. Sent to
individual and IRS at end of tax year.

Form 5304-SIMPLE
Savings Incentive Match Plan for Employees.
(not subject to the designated financial institution rules)
IRS prototype plan agreement.

Form 5305
Individual Retirement Trust Account
IRS prototype trust account agreement. Used by trustee to
establish IRA trust. Typically trustee has information on form
inserted into a company pamphlet.

Form 5305-A
Individual Retirement Custodial Account
IRS prototype custodial account agreement.

Form 5305-R
Roth Individual Retirement Trust Account
IRS prototype trust account agreement.

Form 5305-S
SIMPLE Individual Retirement Trust Account
IRS prototype trust account agreement.

Form 5305-SA
SIMPLE Individual Retirement Custodial Account
IRS prototype custodial account agreement.

Form 5305-SEP
Simplified Employee Pension - Individual Retirement Accounts Contribution Agreement
IRS prototype trust account agreement.

Form 5305-SIMPLE
Savings Incentive Match Plan for Employees
IRS prototype plan agreement.

Form 5329
Additional Taxes Attributable to Qualified Retirement Plans
Used by individuals to identify and calculate additional taxes owed (penalty) due to early withdrawals or excess contributions to retirement plans.

Form 5498
IRA Contribution Information
Used by trustee to identify IRA contributions from an individual. Sent to individual at end of tax year.

Form 8606
Nondeductible IRA's
Used by individuals to keep track of nontaxable IRA contributions. Maintains basis for determining nontaxable portion of withdrawal. Must be filed any year contribution or distribution of nondeductible funds is made.

Form 5305A-SEP
Salary Reduction and Other Elective Simplified Employee Pension - Individual Retirement Accounts Contribution Agreement
IRS prototype trust account agreement.

Publication 575
Pension and Annuity Income
IRS information on pension and annuity income for individuals receiving disbursements.

Publication 590
Individual Retirement Arrangements
IRS explanation and information on IRA's.

Publication 939
General Rules for Pension and Annuities
IRS general rules for pension and annuities. Includes life expectancy tables.

Glossary

10 percent penalty The IRS charges a 10 percent tax penalty referred to as a 10 percent additional tax for early withdrawals from a qualified retirement that do not meet the special criteria established for early withdrawals.

401(k) plan A qualified company sponsored retirement plan that allows employees to defer a portion of their earnings on a tax-deferred basis for the purpose of investing for retirement.

Adjusted Gross Income The AGI is the amount of income after certain additions and deductions to income are accounted for.

agent-to-agent transfer The method used to directly transfer a qualified retirement account from one trustee to another. This method does not allow the investor to get control of the money.

back-end sales load A delayed sales fee taken out when the funds in a mutual fund are taken out of the fund.

beneficiary A person eligible to receive your IRA benefits when you die.

capital gain The realization of capital appreciation when an investment is sold.

cash flow Money available from earnings after taking into account expenses. This could be a positive or negative number.

commingled IRA account An IRA that contains both money rolled over from a qualified company retirement plan and money contributed by the IRA owner.

conduit IRA An IRA that contains only moneys associated with a rollover from a qualified company retirement plan.

continual sales load A sales load that continues each year for the life of the investment. A common continual sales load is the 12b-1 fee found in some mutual funds.

defined benefit plan A retirement plan that pays a known benefit at retirement. This type of plan is the traditional company pension.

defined contribution plan A retirement plan with a final value based on the contributions to the plan and the investment's performance. The 401(k), ESOP and profit sharing plans are popular examples.

direct transfer A process where an IRA is moved from one trustee to another without the funds being sent to the investor as in a rollover.

discount broker A brokerage that offers a full line of investment products at a discounted price.

The discount is possible because the brokerage does not offer investment advice.

distribution Funds removed from a qualified retirement investment such as an IRA.

diversify To spread investment risk among different asset classes

dividends The payouts of excess company net income to shareholder of stocks. Typically associated with payments for common stock.

earned income Wages, tips, bonuses, and commissions earned by an individual. Items such as investment income and other passive income are not considered earned income.

Educational IRA A special type of IRA designed to save for a child's education.

effective return The equivalent return an investor would achieve if the exempt or deferred tax liability is taken into consideration.

ESOP The Employee Stock Ownership Plan allows companies to set up a qualified retirement plan for employees to purchase company stock. It is a defined contribution plan that invests mainly in company stock.

FIFO The First in First Out (FIFO) method considers the first shares or dollars contributed to an investment as the first ones removed when withdrawals are made.

filing status The IRS categorizes taxpayers by filing status. The general categories are single, married filing jointly, married filing separately and head of household.

first-time home buyer The 1997 Tax Payer Relief Act allows you to avoid the 10 percent withdrawal penalty if the money is used for first-time home buyer expenses. You are considered a first-time home buyer if you had no ownership interest in a principle residence during the last two years.

front end sales load An initial sales fee associated with mutual fund investing. The fee is taken out of the funds of the initial investment.

growth stocks Stock in a company that pays little or no dividends but is expected to grow at a rather rapid pace.

Hope credit A special tax credit for educational expenses incurred during the first two years of college.

income phase-out The range where allowable contribution amounts are phased out for taxpayers.

inflation An increase in overall cost of goods and services. Inflation drives the prices of consumer goods up and decreases the dollar's purchasing power.

interest The payment to lenders for borrowing of capital. Typically associated with bond payments.

investment time horizon The length of time an investor plans to have funds dedicated to a certain investment strategy.

IRA Individual Retirement Arrangement or Account. Insurance products are called Individual Retirement Annuity. A tax deferral retirement investment plan permitted by the IRS for individuals who have earned income. The individual is responsible for setting up and contributing to the plan.

IRA conversion A special method used to change a traditional IRA to a Roth IRA.

IRS interpretive bulletins IRS interpretive bulletins provide specific topic interpretations for tax payers. They are usually focused on a single item and not on a wide subject matter.

IRS publications IRS publications contain information and explanations of the tax law as interpreted by the Internal Revenue Service.

Keogh plan A qualified, tax-deferred plan designed for the self-employed.

life expectancy The estimated time an individual will live based on current age.

lifelong learning credit A tax credit that may be used to offset post secondary educational expenses.

long-term capital gains Realized capital appreciation for investments held for greater than one year.

loophole An unintended event that may be used. It occurs as the result of incorrectly worded or omission of wording in the IRA tax code.

lump sum distribution The receiving of the entire value of one's qualified retirement plan from an employer.

marginal tax rate The incremental tax rates that a taxpayer is subject to based on the amount of taxable income.

minimum withdrawals The minimum amount a traditional IRA investor is required to withdraw from their account based upon certain conditions. Also referred to as mandatory withdrawal.

Modified Adjusted Gross Income (MAGI) An investor's adjusted gross income with certain additions as required by the tax law. IRA deductibility uses MAGI to determine eligibility. See Appendix A.

money market fund A fund that invests entirely in cash equivalents. The fund may be taxable or tax exempt.

mutual fund Investment money pooled together by individual investors and managed by a professional

fund manager.

no-load mutual fund A special type of mutual fund that does not charge a sales commission or sales load.

ordinary income All income received by an individual except long-term capital gains.

pension A defined benefit provided by a company for an employee. The company typically funds the pension investment.

phase-out ranges The income ranges where eligibility for contributions to an IRA are reduced to zero.

portfolio The sum total of all investments held by an individual.

private letter rulings The IRS may issue private letter rulings to tax payers on specific situations unique to the tax payer and not explicit in publications and interpretive bulletins.

profit sharing plan A contribution plan where employers make contributions on behalf of employees to an account set up for the employee.

qualified retirement plan A retirement plan that is structured under IRS guidelines and qualifies for special tax treatment.

rollover The process of moving funds from one qualified retirement account to another without losing tax deferral.

rollover paid to you When your account is liquidated and the money is sent to you. If it is from a company qualified plan it will have 20 percent of funds withheld for income taxes. The IRA's do not withhold taxes during a rollover.

Roth IRA A new type of IRA that requires after-tax contributions and tax-free withdrawals under qualified circumstances.

SARSEP A special type of SEP known as a Salary Reduction Simplified Employee Pension that allows for employee deferrals of salary into a IRA.

Self-Directed IRA The common name of an IRA where the owner selects their own investments from an available selection.

SEP Simplified Employee Pension. A qualified retirement plan for small businesses and for the self-employed. The plan has simplified administrative requirements which makes it attractive to small employers.

Simple IRA Saving Incentive Match Plan for Employees. New retirement plan designated for companies with fewer than 100 employees. It is designed to simplify paperwork and requirements for small businesses.

spousal IRA An IRA established for a non-working

spouse where contributions are made from the working spouse's earned income.

substantially equal distributions   A process of receiving a distribution from an IRA based on a yearly calculation using the account value and life expectancy of the investor. The payments are not actually the same each year.

tax bracket   The IRS defined bracket based on income level for a taxpayer.

tax deductible   Income to an individual that is deductible from taxes due to certain qualified uses of the money.

tax free   Income to an individual that would normally be taxed but under certain circumstances is not taxed.

tax-deferred   A tax-deferred investment is one where the investment gains are not taxed in the year they are made but deferred to some future time, typically retirement. Taxes are due when the money is withdrawn.

tax-exempt   A tax-exempt investment is one where the interest return is not subject to federal and possible state or local taxes.

total return   Dividends, interest or other income received from an investment, plus or minus capital appreciation or loss.

traditional IRA   An IRA that allows for either tax deductible or non-deductible contributions and deferral of investment gains until withdrawn.

trustee   A person or agency who is responsible for the handling of an individual or organization's assets.

All About the New IRA

Index

Symbols

1997 Tax Payer Relief Act
11, 13, 19, 28
401(k) 85, 121

A

Adjusted Gross Income (AGI) 123
administration fees 40
amortization method 30

B

banks 38
benchmark returns 110
beneficiary 36, 52
    Educational IRA 70, 73, 75
borrowing from a retirement vehicle 108
brokerage houses 39

C

capital gains 55, 67
commingled account 27
conduit IRA 27
contributions 19
    eligibility 19
    examples 21
    IRS filing date 25
    paying taxes 26
    to a conduit IRA 27
conversions 50, 97
    taxes 50
credit unions 38

D

deferred income 123
defined-contribution plan 119
direct transfer 35
distributions
    age 70 1/2 years and older 31
    before age 59 1/2 29
    between age 59 1/2 and 70 1/2 31
    calculating 30
    Educational IRA 72
    from a Roth IRA 48
    penalties 28
    substantially equal 30
Dogs of the Dow 55

E

early retirement 29
Educational IRA
    definition 69
    eligibility 71
    features 70
    how to start 81
    qualified expenses 72
estate planning 36, 52

F

first-time home buyer 28

I

inflation hedge 66
insurance companies 38

investment choices 37
IRA deductible eligibility 128
IRA, definition 15
IRS form 1040 123
IRS form 1099-R 27
IRS form 5035-R 54
IRS form 8606 26

L

life expectancy method 30, 32

M

MAGI 128
marginal tax rate 87, 126
minimum distributions
    Roth IRA 49, 54
minimum withdrawal calculation
30
money market 109
mutual fund 39, 113

N

non-deductible IRA 17

P

penalties 12
    Roth IRA withdrawals 49
personal income tax 123

Q

qualified
    distributions from Roth IRA 48
    educational expense 28, 72
    educational institution 28
    family member 29

R

responsibilities of IRA investor 38
rollover 27, 35, 116
    Educational IRA 74
Roth IRA
    advantages 44
    basic features 45
    benefits 65
    contributions 46
    conversions 50
    distributions 48
    eligibility 45
    estate planning 52
    rollovers 49
    spousal contribution 46
    state taxes 53

S

self-directed IRA 38
SIMPLE plan 121
spousal beneficiary 36
spousal IRA 11
starting an IRA 38
state taxes 53

T

tax deferral 109
tax-deferred 16, 87
tax-exempt bonds 109
taxes
    and investing 123
    diversifying 54, 66
    tracking taxes owed 26
transfering money
    best method 35
trust account 36

V

variable annuity 110

W

withdrawal penalties 29, 34

Also by Steve Merritt

Information Reports

What to Do With Your Retirement Account When You Leave the Company..$12

All About Self-Directed IRA Investing..$12

All About Variable Annuity Investing..$12

Street Smart Investing; *A behind-the-scenes look at sales tactics used in the industry*..$10

Books

How to Build Wealth with your 401(k) : *Everything you need to know to become more than a millionaire over the course of your working life-time*..$19.95

Investor's Resource Guide : *Hard-to-Find information at your finger-tips*..$12.95

To order, send check or money order along with your request to **Halyard Press, Inc., Orders Dept., P.O. Box 410308, Melbourne, FL 32941**. Shipping and handling is <u>free</u>. Please add 6 percent sales tax for reports shipped to Florida addresses.

About the National Association of 401(k) Investors

The National Association of 401(k) Investors is a nonprofit, public education organization that teaches people how to invest in 401(k) and similar retirement plans. Membership is $39 per year and includes a one-year subscription to the *401(k) Journal,* unlimited use of the Q&A Infoline, and a free copy of *How to Build Wealth with your 401(k)* (a 188 page book valued at $19.95). You also get discounts on other information sources including a professionally prepared analysis of your own 401(k) investments. For more information, call **(407) 636-5737**. To join, send a check or money order for $39 to **National Association of 401(k) Investors, Membership Services, P.O. Box 410755, Melbourne, FL 32941.**